Rosie and the Bad, Bad Apples

A Children's Musical

Valerie Hall

A Samuel French Acting Edition

SAMUELFRENCH-LONDON.CO.UK
SAMUELFRENCH.COM

ROSIE AND THE BAD, BAD APPLES

Rosie and the Bad, Bad Apples was first presented at The Ilkley Playhouse, Wharfeside Theatre on 25th January 1999, with the following cast:

THE BAD APPLES
Bad Grub	Antony Matthews
Fly-Blow	Alistair Mason
Bruiser	Alistaire MacGregor
Rhoda Russett	Charlotte Green
Rufus Russett	Philip Street
Gardener	Lilia Palmer

APPLE GUESTS
Lady Worcester-Pearmain	Lauren Hird
Twin	Emily E. Thirlwell
Twin	Frances Kroon
Delia	Rosie Greaves
Ida	Chloe Seddon
Baby Rosie Russet	Gail Mawdsley
Mr Crispin (later Professor Crispin)	Peter Zezulka
Crispin's Pal in the band	James Kitching
Crispin's other Pal	Chloe Hampson
The Pieman	Mike Denby
Granny Smith	Julia Wilson
Rosie Russet, as a young girl	Hannah Kew
Polly Pippin	Karenna Wood
Amelia Crabapple	Sarah Allen
Council Workapple	Andrew Matthews
Sergeant Bramley	Tom Hebbert
Constable Bramley	Danny Horn
Herr Stroodle	Deni Bykem
Barker	Chloe Seddon
Gypsy Appolina	Anna Lambert
Mrs Buzzy Bee	Maria Soundry
Miss Buzzy Bee	Emma Birtwhistle
Young Buzzy Bee	Gail Mawdsley
Giant Honeycake	Katy Balinger
Giant Pie	Lauren Hird

Bessie	Jenny Atkins
Cora	Jennifer Stoddart
Minnie	Emily Strange
Tommy	Jonathon Greaves
Bob	Andrew Matthews

American Tourist	Chloe Seddon

APPLE GUESTS, URCHIN APPLES, ORPHAN APPLES, SPOOKS, MAGGOTS
Danny Horn, Emily Strange,Tom Hebbert, Emily Evans Thirlwell, Louise Kitching, Maria Soundy, Rosie Greaves, James Kitching, Stephanie Kay, Sarah Pearson, Emma Birtwhistle, Lila Palmer, Stacy Hardcastle, Frances Kroon, Daisy Argyle, Frances Taylor, Jennifer Stoddart, Laura Bunn, Joanna Greenwood, Tom Cowley, Anna Lambert, Katy Ballinger, Jessica Wood, Jenny Atkins, Tess Seddon, Jonathan Greaves, Nicola Mason.

Directed by Pat Dyson and Sheila Wright
Set designed by Dooley Coleman
Lighting designed by Richard Speight and Adam Welch
Sound designed by Jack Smethhurst

CHARACTERS

PRINCIPALS
Fly-Blow
Bruiser } The Bad Apples
Bad Grub
Rhoda Russet
Rufus Russet
Rosie Russet, as a baby apple
Rosie Russet, as a young girl
The Pieman
Mr (later Professor) Crispin
Granny Smith, an apple from "Down Under"
Polly Pippin
Amelia Crabapple
Sergeant Bramley
Constable Bramley

CHORUS
Party Guests
Bramleyville Townsfolk
Gardener
Lady Worcester-Pearmain
Bessie
Bob
Giant Honeycake
Giant Pie
Fairground Barker
Mrs Buzzybee
Mrs Buzzybee's Helper
Tourist
Maggots
Urchins
Orphans
Spooks
Fairgoers

SYNOPSIS OF SCENES

ACT I

ACT II

SONGS

ACT I

I	Overture	
1.	**It's a Perfect Day (For a Party)**	Company
2.	**She's Not There**	Bad Apples, Urchins
3.	**The Bad Apple Rap**	Bad Apples, Rosie
4.	**The Happy Apple Song**	Company

ACT II

II.	Entr'acte	
5.	**A Friend Like You**	Rosie, Polly
6.	**Don't Sleep in Hallowe'en Wood Tonight**	Spooks
7.	**Mine!**	Amelia
8.	**Poonaworra**	Granny, Bruiser, Bad Apples
9.	**It's a Perfect Day (For a Party)** (Reprise)	Sergeant, Constable
III.	Finale & Exit Music	Company
	The Happy Apple Song (Reprise)	

A piano/vocal score for the above songs and incidental music is on hire from Samuel French Ltd. Perusal material including a CD of extracts of the original cast recording is available.

A CD is available from the composer for directors wishing to use backing tracks instead of the piano/vocal arrangement. Please enquire through Samuel French Ltd.

PRODUCTION NOTES

This piece should be staged as simply as possible whilst keeping it bright, colourful and comic to the eye.

It is not essential for the actors to be made to look like real apples in cumbersome costumes which would be awkward to perform in — better to aim for a degree of "chubbiness" with no waistlines. Younger cast members could wear loose T-shirts and tights. The Maggots in ACT II could be similarly dressed, but in flesh tones. The apples could have leaves worn around the neck or incorporated into headgear.

The original production was set on an open stage decorated with greenery. Three small revolves were used to highlight the different places visited by Rosie on her travels. They were re-set for three more locations in ACT II. The gloomy "Maggot Marshes" were created by using lengths of floaty grey material, held each end by Maggots, which rippled gently as Rosie and the Bad Apples picked their way precariously across the marsh.

Ideally, the pieman, Granny Smith and Amelia Crabapple should be played by adults, although this play could easily be done by an all youth group. Having a tall actor playing the pieman is also an advantage. However, height is less important than the ability to terrify the unfortunate apples.

Valerie Hall

ACT ONE

Scene 1

On The Way To A Party At Russet Manor

I. Overture

A party is about to take place. There are decorations and a table set with delicious food. (Although if the latter proves impractical waiters or waitresses could bring on trays of refreshments later in this scene). The most important feature is a decorated apple tree, which bears one large fruit — an apple the size of a very large pumpkin. Under the tree is a basket with a frilly cushion

Party guests, apples dressed in their best, some carrying gaily wrapped gifts, enter. They greet each other cheerily and chatter excitedly at the prospect of going to a very special party on what seems to be a perfect day

Song No.1: It's A Perfect Day (For A Party)

Company (*singing*) It's a perfect day for a party,
You couldn't pick a better day.
And we would swear that
Something in the air had
Put us in a mood for celebrating.
Even the sun is shining down as if to say, "Hey! —
This is a perfect day for a party.
Go out and have a party today."

It's a day for being happy,
Not for being glum.
A smile's your invitation
To come and join the fun,
Ev'ryone.

It's a perfect day for making merry,
And apples love to merry-make.
We're the kind you're likely to find
Anywhere there's decorations and a cake.
This party feeling that we're feeling's no mistake,
'Cos, we're really on our way to a party,
And it's a perfect day for a party.
So if you've nothing better to do — why not stay ——

During the following, the apples gradually leave, until there is only one apple left on the stage

(*Singing*) For the party today,
(Party today)
Perfect day
(Perfect day)
For a party today

Last apple   What a day!

The last apple exits

The Bad Apples enter. These are a rascally trio of grunge-clad, wannabe rock stars who spell trouble. Bad Grub, their leader, is a cocky opportunist; Fly-Blow is one of life's grumblers, and Bruiser, who is the biggest, but not the brightest, of the bunch. If possible, they should enter noisily from the auditorium, and provoke the audience with remarks like "You looking at me?", "Come on, if you think you're hard enough", etc.

Two gift-carrying guests, late for the party, enter, hurry past the Bad Apples, and exit

Fly-Blow Looks like there's a party going on somewhere, Bad Grub.
Bad Grub Yeah, I think you could be right.
Bruiser A party?! Ah, I've never been to a party.
Bad Grub You haven't? In that case — (*he crooks an elbow inviting Bruiser to take his arm*) — h'allow me to h'escort you to your first.

Bruiser goes all coy as he takes Bad Grub's arm. Then he stops

Bruiser But, Bad Grub, we haven't been invited.
Bad Grub (*with feigned disappointment*) You're right, Bruiser, we haven't. (*He winks at Fly-Blow*) But we've never let that stop us before, have we, Fly-Blow? Come on lads, it's party time!

The Bad Apples exit in high spirits

The garden at Russet Manor, where the party is to take place

Rufus and Rhoda Russet, the apples of good stock, enter. They are accompanied by a Gardener carrying a watering-can. He wears an apron, with a pair of secateurs and a pair of gardening gloves in the front pocket. He is a somewhat mystical figure. He puts the watering-can down, goes to the tree and gently fusses over the apple growing on it

Party guests start to arrive and are greeted by their hosts, Rufus and Rhoda. There are small exchanges of conversation before the guests move off to form groups. Next, two or three college types arrive, including Mr Crispin. They are wearing blazers, carrying instruments (guitars etc. shaped like apple cores) and a music case, as they are due to play at this party

The Bad Apples enter. The wander about and give "hard stares" to anyone who dares to look at them

Rhoda Rufus, who are those rather unsavoury looking apples? They certainly weren't on my guest list.
Rufus Nor mine, Rhoda dear, I assure you.
Rhoda Well, someone must have asked them.

The Russets' and the Bad Apples' eyes meet. The Russets politely nod and turn away

Rufus (*nervously*) Should I ask to see their invitations d'you think?
Rhoda No, Rufus, let them stay — as long as they behave themselves and don't do anything to spoil our lovely day.

Lady Worcester-Pearmain, an apple of very, very good stock, enters. She carries a gift

Now there's someone who most definitely was on my guest list. Lady Worcester-Pearmain, what an honour it is to have you here.

The Russets and Lady Worcester-Pearmain move away

Fly-Blow This isn't much of a party, Bad Grub. There's no music, no dancing and everyone's just standing round talking.
Bad Grub What d'you expect at a "Picking Party"?
Fly-Blow A "Picking Party"? Of course it is, I should've guessed. We might as well go. I mean, it's hardly going to turn into a rave is it?

Fly-Blow and Bad Grub make to go

Bruiser Here hang on. What's a "Picking Party"?
Fly-Blow Don't you know anything?
Bad Grub D'you mean to say you've never heard of "Picking Parties"?

Bruiser shakes his head

Didn't anyone tell you the facts of life?

*Bruiser shakes his head. Bad Grub gives a long-suffering look then puts a
paternal arm around Bruiser*

> When two apples want a baby apple they go to their tree — their "family
> tree"—and they say, "Please Tree, we'd like to have a baby, will you help
> us?"

Bruiser And what does the tree say?

Bad Grub (*giving another long-suffering look*) Bruiser, trees don't talk.
Anyway, they wait until one day a tiny apple appears on the tree. And they
watch it grow and grow and get bigger and bigger until it's big enough to
be picked. Then they have this party and everyone brings presents and says
what a lovely baby apple it is, even if it's the most horrible baby apple in
Appledom.

Bruiser is clearly enchanted with this story

Bruiser Ah, is that how we all got here?

Fly-Blow Me and Bad Grub maybe, but I don't think anyone would've
picked you. I expect you hung around on the tree 'till you got so big and
so heavy — you just dropped off.

*The Gardener leaves the tree, goes over to the Russets and exchanges a few
words with them. The guests become quiet, aware that something important
is about to happen*

Bruiser Why wouldn't I get "picked"?

Fly-Blow Put it this way, Bruiser, you wouldn't win a "Miss Beautiful
Apple" contest now would you?

Bruiser thinks for a moment

Bruiser (*speaking rather too loudly*) Course not, Fly-Blow. I'm not a girl,
am I?

All the guests turn to look at Bruiser

Guests Shh!

*Rufus takes his wife's arm and they follow the Gardener to the tree. The
Gardener dons the pair of gardening gloves and takes the secateurs from his
apron pocket*

Rhoda (*gently stroking the apple*) Look, Rufus, it has your cheeks.

Rufus And your beautiful skin.

The Russets nod to the Gardener who ceremoniously cuts the stem by which the apple is attached to the tree. The Russets put their hands underneath the apple as it comes away from the tree, to support its weight. All the guests hold their breath as the new baby apple is carefully lowered onto the frilly cushion in the basket. There are a couple of leaves around the stem which the gardener lifts to look underneath

Bruiser is entranced by all this. Not so are his friends

Gardener It's a girl!

The Russets are delighted. The guests let out a collective "Aah!" The Gardener clears his/her throat to indicate that everyone should be quiet

Now, repeat after me. We solemnly swear.

Rufus
Rhoda } We solemnly swear.

Gardener That we will cherish this apple.

Rufus
Rhoda } That we will cherish this apple.

Gardener Cultivate her.

Rufus
Rhoda } Cultivate her.

Gardener And protect her from blight as long as we both shall live.

Rufus
Rhoda } And protect her from blight as long as we both shall live.

Gardener And what is she to be called?

Rufus
Rhoda } (*looking at each other*) Rosie.

The Gardener takes a label from his pocket and writes on it

Gardener I name this apple, Rosie, of the family Russet.

*The Gardener ties the label to Rosie's stem. Then he/she picks up the watering-can and waters the apple with a silvery dust. This is accompanied by some tinkly music to give the procedure a magic feel (**No.1a.**)*

The Russets and the Gardener then mask the apple so that a small child, Rosie, in similar costume can take the apple's place. They move aside and Rosie stretches out first one arm then the other

The Gardener turns the basket around to face the audience

Rhoda She's beautiful. She's the most beautiful Rosie Russet that ever was picked.
Rufus Yes, she's the sweetest baby apple in the whole of Appledom.

The Russets take a hand each and help Rosie off her cushion. She is wobbly, like a young animal. There are appropriate "Oohs" and "Aahs" from the guests as Rosie is guided to c. Lady Worcester-Pearmain crosses to them, carrying her gift. She is followed by two more guests. The second guest is a rather dour apple

Bad Grub and Fly-Blow are somewhat nauseated by the proceedings

Lady (*presenting her gift*) May she be blessed with a sweet nature and a pure and honest core.
1st Guest May she grow to be plump of flesh and shiny of skin.
2nd Guest May she never be troubled by mildew or worms.
Rufus I too have a gift for our child. It's rather special. (*He takes a locket and chain from his pocket and shows it to his wife. He opens the locket which contains pictures of the two of them*)
Rhoda Oh, Rufus, it's us! Little tiny pictures of you and me. How sweet.
Rufus (*placing the chain over Rosie's head*) It's so she won't forget us, Rhoda. One day, in the future when we're no longer here, she'll look at this and remember how much we loved her.
Rhoda Don't be so gloomy, Rufus, you're making me feel sad. We'll always be together won't we, Rosie? We'll never let you out of our sight. Now why don't you make your little speech so that we can get on with the party.
Rufus Yes, dear. (*He clears his throat*) My wife and I want to thank you all for your generous gifts and good wishes for Rosie's future. She couldn't have a better start in life. Now — let the merry-making begin.

Mr Crispin frantically rummages in his music case. Rhoda, noticing that something is wrong, nudges her husband

Eat, drink and dance the night away. Over to you, Mr Crispin.

He gestures, without looking, to where Crispin and his friends should be ready to play

Over to you, Mr Crisp ... What is it, Rhoda?

A rather embarrassed Mr Crispin moves towards Rufus and Rhoda

Crispin I'm so dreadfully sorry, but I seem to have forgotten the music and
we can't play without it.
Rhoda I said we should have hired a proper band and not a handful of
students. This is all your fault ——

The Russets start to argue. Bad Grub turns excitedly to his pals

Bad Grub D'you hear that? The band's forgotten its music. "Can't play
without it". This could be our chance to make a name for ourselves.
Fly-Blow You mean, us — play?
Bad Grub Why not? Look around — I reckon there are some pretty
important apples here who could help us to get our career off the ground.
Come on, let's get this party moving.

*Bad Grub, Fly-Blow and Bruiser rush across and grab the guitar etc. from
Mr Crispin and his friends. Then they break into some very heavy metal. The
Russets are stunned and the Guests cover their ears*

Song No.1b: Bad Apples Main Theme

Bad Apples   (*Singing*) We're the Bad Apples
We're the Bad Apples, yeah!
We're the Bad Apples,
'Cos we don't like being good.

Bad Grub This is more like it. We're shaking it up now, lads.
Fly-Blow Yeah, things are really moving.

*We hear heavy footsteps approaching and the Lighting becomes dark. The
ground trembles*

The Guests become alarmed. Bruiser looks puzzled

Bruiser 'Ere, Fly-Blow, things really are moving.
Fly-Blow }
Bad Grub } (*together*) What?!

A big shadow appears

The party comes to a sudden halt

Bad Apples Whooa!!!

The Bad Apples hide where they can observe the following action

The guests take a line each during the following

Guests What is it? What's happening?

We hear evil laughter

No! It can't be. Surely not. But it is, I'm sure it is. Who? Who is it? It's him. The Pieman!

The Pieman enters. A tall man who should be a giant to the apples. He wears chef's clothing — an apron and a chef's hat that gives him extra height. An outsized corer/peeler hangs from his belt. He is charming. When he becomes angry this charm makes him more frightening

Pieman Yes, it's me. My invitation get lost in the post did it? Never mind, I'm here now. I knew you wouldn't want me to miss out on such an important occasion. You know how I love Picking Parties.(*He sees the food table*) My what a spread. Hard to know what to choose first.

Rufus edges towards the food whist trying to shield his wife and child

Rufus W...w...what do you want?
Pieman What do you think I want?
Rufus How about a honeycake? I believe they're delicious.
Pieman Too sticky. Try again.
Rufus (*with desperation*) Some jelly perhaps?
Pieman Nasty wobbly stuff. Come now, let's stop playing games. You know perfectly well what I want, what I always want, what I'm famous for wanting.
Rufus We don't have any pies.
Pieman No? Oh dear. Then I'll just have to make my own. (*From his apron pocket he produces a large pastry shell*)

Gasps of horror come from the Apple Guests

Now, what to put in it? (*He looks around and spots Rosie*) Ah! (*Pointing to Rosie*) That looks tasty. Fresh too.
Rufus (*with anguish*) No!!!
Rhoda Rufus! Do something! That — monster wants to take our Rosie.

The Pieman seems a trifle offended at being called a monster. Rufus tries to placate him

Rufus Look here, old chap, let's be practical. Rosie's only a baby, just picked. She'd hardly fill a dumpling let alone a whole pie. (*He swallows hard*) Take me instead.

Rhoda Rufus, no!!!

Pieman Don't worry, madam, you can keep him, he's way past his best. I prefer my pie filling to be young and tender — it cooks quicker.

While the Pieman expounds on the best way to cook a pie, Rhoda decides to take matters into her own hands and begins to tip-toe towards the tree indicating to the Gardener that he/she should join her

Of course I may allow her to mature a little so that her natural flavour can develop — Hey! What d'you think you're doing?

Rhoda Putting Rosie back on the tree, you can't touch her there. (*She wipes a finger over the tip of Rosie's stem*) See, the sap's still flowing. We can graft her back on.

Pieman Oh you don't stop me that easily. Two can play at that game.

Rufus What do you mean?

Pieman You'll see. (*He purses his lips and blows*)

The Pieman creates a strong wind and blossoms swirl about like snow

Some of the Guests are blown off stage, others run away

The Russets try to hold on to Rosie, but she is wrenched from their grasp. With arms flailing, she whirls about. Mr Crispin tries to help the Russets catch their child. The Pieman waits until they are just about to grab Rosie, then he blows her in another direction

With one almighty puff the Pieman blows the young apple off stage

Her parents watch as if she is climbing up into the sky

Rufus (*in disbelief*) She's — flying.

Rhoda (*with anguish*) Rosie! Rosie!

Rhoda rushes off stage

Rufus Rhoda, come back. It's no use.

Rufius rushes after his wife

Crispin My dear friends.

Mr Crispin runs after them. The Pieman exits, laughing

The stage is empty. The party that started so perfectly is now a shambles. The Bad Apples peep out to see if the coast is clear, then emerge from their hiding place

Bad Grub Wow! That was awesome. What does he do for an encore?
Fly-Blow } *(together)* Huh?
Bruiser }
Bad Grub What a dude! Did you see how he blew everything away? Sheer chaos. Unbelievable. Wouldn't it be great if we could get him for one of our gigs?

The Pieman's shadow starts to appear

Fly-Blow tries to signal the shadow to Bad Grub, but he is too carried away to pay attention

That'd really get our career off the ground. He could be our support act — and carry our equipment too — that's when we get some equipment.

The Pieman enters

Pieman Think I'm a dude, do you?

Bad Grub nearly jumps out of his skin

Like to book me for one of your gigs would you? Have me carry your equipment too. Why you pathetic little pipsqueak, I should skin you alive and fry you up for fritters — all of you. (*He brandishes the apple peeler*)
Bad Grub Please Mr Pieman, sir, don't do that. We wouldn't taste very nice I assure you. We ain't what you'd call the pick of the crop, are we? Take Bruiser here. (*He pulls Bruiser forward*) Look at him. By the time you'd peeled away his skin and cut out all his nasty bits, you'd have nothing left.

Bruiser faints

Pieman You have a point. You're certainly not the most appetising bunch, not like that apple I just blew away. She would have made top quality pie filling.

The Bad Apples try to slip away

Oh no you don't. You come back here, I want you to do something for me.

Bad Grub Anything you say, your Piedish ... er ... Pieshop ...er ... Mr
  Pieman.
Pieman I want you to find that apple, that Rosie, and bring her to me.
Bad Grub Yes, well, there could be a bit of a problem with that.
Pieman There'd better not be.
Bad Grub Be fair, sir, we don't know where she'll be.
Pieman Of course you don't, and neither do I, that's why I'm asking you to
  look for her.
Fly-Blow It could take ages, she might be anywhere by now.
Pieman I can wait. In a season or two she'll have grown plumper, crisper,
  sweeter. The perfect apple for the perfect pie. Well, don't just stand there,
  make a start.

*The Bad Apples start to go, but then Fly-Blow whispers something to Bad
Grub. Bad Grub summons up all his courage to face the Pieman*

Bad Grub One more thing.
Pieman Ye — es?
Bad Grub What's in it for us?
Pieman What?!
Bad Grub I mean, we're going to have to put our career on hold while we
  run around looking for this apple. And then there's bound to be expenses.
  Accommodation, transportation ——
Pieman Enough! Do a good job and you'll get your reward. But think on this,
  I'll have a pie dish ready and waiting and if you don't bring me Rosie to
  fill it — then guess who will have to take her place?
Bad Apples Us?
Pieman Exactly.

The Pieman exits

Fly-Blow What we gonna do, BG?
Bad Grub Do? We do like he says, we find Rosie.
Bruiser But what if we don't find her? He said he'd put us in a pie dish. I don't
  want to be put in a pie dish. I don't even like wearing a vest. (*He snivels*)
  I want to go home.
Bad Grub You ain't got no home, Bruiser. So pull yourself together and let's
  get cracking. Now, which way did she blow?
Fly-Blow }
Bruiser } (*together, pointing different ways*) That way.
Bad Grub Great! Well I say — this way. Come on.

*Bad Grub, Fly-Blow and Bruiser exit. As they go they sing the "Bad
Apples" theme, but in a rather subdued way* (**No.1c. & 1d. underscore**)

SCENE 2

A LONG WAY FROM RUSSET MANOR

Granny Smith enters. She is is an apple of antipodean origin. She is rough, tough, but with a heart of gold. She is on her way back to her cottage and could enter from the auditorium and make her way up onto the stage. It is raining and she carries an umbrella with corks hanging from it, like the Australian hats. She grumbles to herself

Granny Bloomin' Pommie weather! I'll never get used to it. One minute it's raining ——

A strong wind starts to blow

— then it's blowing a gale. Whatever next? Snow?!

The wind gets stronger and Granny has trouble controlling her brolly. She gets blown about the stage

Oh! Oh! Oh!

Rosie enters, carried here by the Pieman's breath

Granny and Rosie are whirled around until the wind dies down. They both flop down onto the ground next to, but unaware of each other. Granny turns her head and sees Rosie and nearly jumps out of her skin

What the …? (*She examines Rosie closely*) Chop me up and call me puree, if it isn't a bloomin' baby!

Rosie begins to cry

No need for tears, Granny Smith won't hurt you. My, you're a young'un and no mistake. (*She sniffs Rosie*) Only just picked by the smell of you. (*She looks at Rosie's label*) Rosie. So that's your name. You're a long way from home, Rosie. There's not another apple within miles of this place. (*She opens the locket*) Are these your old'uns? They're a bonzer looking pair. Good apples I reckon. Something mighty strange must've happened to have parted you from them. Still... (*she rises*) I expect they'll come looking for you soon enough, but would you like to bunk down with old Granny Smith until they do? You would?

Granny helps Rosie up and they move towards the wings

Did I ever tell you about the time when I won the county arm wrestling contest, back home in Poonaworra? I didn't? Well, there was this big, hairy apple from Digger Valley…

Granny and Rosie exit

We leave Rosie for a while so that she can do some growing, carefully tended by Granny, and go to:

Scene 3

Looking For Rosie

A group of scruffy urchin apples sit around, playing. Nearby, are two large rustic-looking dustbins. One of the dustbins is empty. The other dustbin has an urchin hiding inside, plus Bruiser's socks, Bruiser's underwear, a giant A-Z and the Pieman's Bill of Fare that are referred to in the following song

The Bad Apples enter

The Bad Apples have had no luck in tracking down their quarry. They look around as they search for Rosie. Bruiser lifts a dustbin lid and peers in; it is empty. He lifts the other lid and the urchin pops up giving Bruiser a scare. Bruiser scurries over to his friends for protection. The urchins giggle

Bad Grub Any luck, Fly-Blow?
Fly-Blow Nah, nothing.
Bad Grub How about you, Bruiser? Don't suppose you've found her by any chance?
Bruiser Found who, BG?
Bad Grub ⎫
Fly-Blow ⎭ (*together*) Oh, Bruiser!
Urchins Oh, Brui — ser!

Bruiser looks hurt. Fly-Blow explodes in anger

Fly-Blow Rosie! Rosie! That's who. We're looking for her, remember?
Bad Grub Take it easy, he's doing his best.
Fly-Blow But I'm tired of telling him.
Bad Grub We're all tired.

The urchin pulls out each of the props from the dustbin as they are mentioned in the song

Song No 2: She's Not There

Bad Grub	Since that day the Pieman blew her away, We've not had a single moment's rest.
Bad Grub **Fly-Blow** }	Our life's been far from cosy Looking for that Rosie
Bad Grub **Fly-Blow** **Bruiser** }	And finding her could be a fruitless quest. We've looked high, we've looked low We've looked ev'ry place we know, But she's not there. We've looked in villages and towns, Over hills and underground, And she's not there. We've looked in puddles and in ponds, In the back of beyond It's enough to make us swear.
Bad Grub **Fly-Blow** }	We've looked in caves and under rocks, We've even looked in Bruiser's socks. She's not there.

An urchin holds up Bruiser's socks

During the following, the Bad Apples go down into the audience to look for Rosie. They mistake some little girls for her and/or hand out leaflets with an identikit picture on and the words "Have you seen this apple?"

Urchins	They've looked high, they've looked low, They've looked ev'ry place they know, But she's not there. They've looked in villages and towns, Over hills and underground, And she's not there. They've looked in puddles and in ponds, In the back of beyond. It's enough to make them swear. They've searched in wind and rain and snow. In places apples shouldn't go! She's not there.

Bruiser joins the Urchins and they dance with him. A dance in which Bruiser, as usual, is made to look foolish. Eventually, Bad Grub and Fly-Blow make their way back onto the stage

| **Bad Grub** | Seasons come, seasons go
And still Rosie doesn't show
Anywhere. |

Bad Grub
Fly-Blow } We never rest, we hardly eat.
Bruiser   We've aching heads and tired feet.

Bruiser } And no clean underwear!
Bad grub } According to this book —

An urchin holds up the A-Z, and Bruiser's underwear

There's only one place left to look

All Three   And if she isn't there — (*speaking*) well,
(*Singing*) Here's a thought that's not too cheering,
Guess who soon will be appearing
On the Pieman's Bill of Fare?

An urchin holds up a Bill of Fare

Bruiser   Will she be there? (*He points to a child in the audience*)
Will she be there? (*He points to another child in the audience*)

Bad Apples } No! We'll/they'll be there!
Urchins }

We hear the sound of the Pieman's footsteps. Everyone freezes

Bad Grub We'd better get out of here!

The Bad Apples and the urchins scarper off stage

Music continues to underscore (**No. 2a.**)

SCENE 4

GRANNY SMITH'S COTTAGE

The outside of Granny Smith's Cottage

It is a somewhat scruffy exterior with garden tools and a large object, wrapped in sacking, propped up against the wall. There is an old chair, beside which is a basket, full of boomerangs which Granny has whittled

A simple barbecue is gently smoking

Granny Smith and Rosie come out from inside the cottage. Several seasons have passed since Rosie blew into Granny's life. Rosie now looks about fourteen to fifteen years old in human years; not pretty, but pleasant with obvious good breeding, inherited from her parents. She has a certain stubbornness learned from Granny Smith. Rosie carries a tray of food which she puts down near the barbecue, and then puts the food on the fire to cook. Granny watches, somewhat concerned as she smokes on a corn-cob pipe

Granny Struth, Rosie, you be careful with that. You don't want to go burning yourself. P'raps I'd better do it.
Rosie Thank you, granny, but I can manage. I'm a big apple now you know.

Granny sits, takes a half finished boomerang from the basket and whittles away at it

Granny I suppose you are. Seems like only yesterday you fell out the bloomin' sky and nearly scared me out of my skin.
Rosie And you took me in and brought me up and taught me everything I know.
Granny Yeah, except I could never teach you to talk proper, like me.

Rosie fingers her locket and looks thoughtful

Rosie I suppose my parents must've stopped looking for me by now, that's if they bothered to in the first place.
Granny Don't go talking that way, blossom.

Granny gestures to Rosie to come and sit by her

I reckon they loved you a lot, but whatever blew you here was mighty powerful and we don't know how far you travelled. There could be an awful lot of places to look between where you started off and where you landed, so don't give up hope yet.
Rosie Granny, there's something I want to talk to you about. Something I've been thinking about a lot lately. Please don't think I'm not grateful for everything that you've done for me , but ——
Granny But you want to go looking for your old'uns, don't you?
Rosie How did you guess?
Granny I've always known that if they didn't find you first one day you'd want to go looking for them. It's only natural you wanting to be with your own flesh and juice.

Rosie Thank you for understanding. (*She hugs Granny*) I'll come back as soon as I've found them I promise, and I'll bring them with me, they'll be bound to want to meet you.

Granny I'm sure they will. Hey, I thought you were in charge of the barbie. Food'll be burnt one side and raw on the other if you don't turn it over.

Rosie moves to tend to the barbecue

Before you go looking for your old'uns, Rosie, there's something I gotta tell you. Something important that you must know.

Rosie Ooh, this sounds serious.

Granny It is serious, so listen hard. (*She pauses*) When you leave here you've got to be careful 'cos it's not always safe for young apples like you. There's danger lurking out there and his name … his name … is the Pieman!

The mere mention of his name has a chilling effect on Rosie

Rosie (*whispering in awe*) The Pieman?

Granny He's as cunning as he's evil and you never know where he'll turn up next. But the worse thing about him is that he turns good apples into bad and makes them do his dirty work for him so you never know who to trust.

Rosie Have you ever seen him?

Granny Once, when I was younger. It was back in Poonaworra, I was out mending a fence when it suddenly got cold and a dark shadow fell across our land.

Rosie What happened?

Granny Well I know evil when I smell it, so I quickly hid under the house. I guess I was so scared I plum forgot about Joey, playing in the yard.

Rosie Joey?

Granny My little brother. When I went to look for him all I found was a long piece of skin.

Rosie You mean …?

Granny Yep. He'd put him in a pie. After that I had to get away. So I packed a few things and caught the next strong wind that came along — that's how I ended up here, living among you Pommie-Apples. But I can't forget what happened, and if that great streak of nastiness ever crosses my path again, I'll be ready for him. (*She is so worked up that she bites the end off her pipe*) Struth! I've got meself so fired up I've bitten me pipe in half. (*She rises*) I'll go and get another.

Granny goes into the cottage

*Rosie turns over the food. In the distance we hear a familiar strain, "We are the Bad Apples". (**No.2b.**) Rosie seems not to hear*

Bad Grub (*off*) Bruiser, you go that way. Me and Fly-Blow'll take this path.
Bruiser (*off*) Aw, Bad Grub, why do I have to be on my own?
Fly-Blow (*off*) Because you haven't washed for days and you pong. So do as BG says and shout if you find her, you know the drill.

Bruiser enters. He is walking backwards, his hand above his eyes as he looks around. Rosie takes a step back and they bump, gasp, turn around and face each other

Bruiser You scared me.
Rosie You scared me too. We don't see many other apples around here.

They look at each other, both at a loss for words

(*Holding out her hand*) I'm Ros …

Bruiser has smelled the barbecue. He moves straight to it, ignoring Rosie

Bruiser What's this?
Rosie (*joining Bruiser*) A barbie. It's a funny way of cooking that Granny taught me. Look, there's honeyburgers, honey chops, honey drumsticks.

Bruiser looks very, very hungry

Would you like to stay for lunch? I'm sure Granny won't mind.
Bruiser Oh yeah, ta. I'm starving. I can't remember when I last ate.
Rosie Poor you. The food's not ready yet, but you can give me a hand while we're waiting.

Rosie shows Bruiser how to turn the food

You haven't told me your name.
Bruiser It's Bruiser.
Rosie (*holding out her hand*) Pleased to meet you, Bruiser. I'm Rosie.

Bruiser scratches his head, thoughtfully

Bruiser Rosie? Rosie? I've heard that name before. (*Slowly, light dawns*) Oh yeah! I'm looking for an apple called Rosie.
Rosie (*excitedly*) You are?!

Bruiser I remember now, it was a long time ago. We was at this party and a baby, this Rosie, got blown away. Someone told us to find her and we've been looking for her ever since.
Rosie (*really excited*) Bruiser, I got blown away when I was a baby.
Bruiser No! That's amazing! Two apples, both called Rosie, both blown away, and I've met — both of them.
Rosie (*with great patience*) No, Bruiser, you don't understand — not two Rosies, just one — me.

Bruiser looks blank

Look, is this who told you to look for Rosie? (*She shows him the pictures in her locket*)
Bruiser Nah, that's nothing like the Pieman.

Bruiser and Rosie stare at each other. Suddenly the penny drops

Rosie The Pieman? Oh no! Granny, help. Come quickly!

Bruiser tries to grab Rosie

Bruiser Bad Grub! Fly-Blow! It's what's-her-name, I've got her. Hurry up!

Rosie escapes from Bruiser and gets behind the barbecue. She throws food at him, which he either eats or puts in his pocket

Granny rushes out of the cottage

Bad Grub and Fly-Blow enter. They are pulling a small wicker cart, which is a mobile cage

Granny grabs her boomerangs and throws them at the Bad Apples. Bad Grub and Fly-Blow cry out lots of "Oohs" and "Ouches"

Rosie They want me for the Pieman, Granny. Don't let them take me.

Alas, Rosie is captured and bundled into the cart

The Bad Apples exit with her, triumphantly singing their theme tune

A distraught Granny stands alone. She straightens her back and lifts her head

Granny (*filled with new resolve*) You got away with it once, Pieman, taking something that was close to my heart, but you won't get away with it this time. Nobody messes with Granny Smith twice and lives to tell the tale. (*She moves to her house and picks up the large wrapped object*) I'm coming after you, Pieman, and this time I'm ready. (*She removes the sacking and holds aloft a giant-sized boomerang*)

*The music underscore (***No. 2c.***) continues*

Black-out

SCENE 5

A CLEARING IN A FOREST

A few hours have passed since Rosie's capture. A young apple called Polly Pippin is collecting sticks of wood. She is a little older than Rosie and is poorly dressed. She hears the Bad Apples in the distance and hides behind a bush from where she observes the action

Bad Grub and Fly-Blow enter. They are in good spirits

Bad Grub (*as a football chant*) Oh, Piema — an. Mr Piema — an.
Fly-Blow Piema — an. Mr Piema — an.

They do this for a while, then get bored

I'm fed up, BG. We spent all that time looking for Rosie and now we've got her we have to start all over again looking for the Pieman.
Bad Grub Cheer up, Fly-Blow, we've done the hard part, now I think we should just stay where we are and let him find us.

They sit

Fly-Blow Yeah, we'll just let him find us. Here, BG, you don't think he'll have forgotten about our reward do you?
Bad Grub Course not. And if he has, I'll have to remind him won't I?
Fly-Blow How much d'you reckon it'll be?
Bad Grub A lot. This has been a long job with loads and loads of expenses. (*He gets out notebook and pencil*) Let's see, there's our travelling expenses.
Fly-Blow But we walked everywhere.
Bad Grub He won't know that. (*Writing in the book*) And there's our accommodation …
Fly-Blow But we slept outside, on the ground.
Bad Grub He won't know that. (*Writing in the book*) Then there's that apple cart, cost a fortune that did.

Fly-Blow But we nicked that from him.
Bad Grub ⎫
Fly-Blow ⎭ (*together*) He'll know that.

Bad Grub rubs out last entry

Fly-Blow How much does it come to?
Bad Grub (*muttering*) Fourteen pounds an hour times ...(*he does some addition on his fingers*) ... number of seasons, plus overtime, plus bonuses, divided by three — that comes to — 50p!
Fly-Blow Each?!

Bad grub nods

Whew, that much. What you gonna do with yours, BG?
Bad Grub Spend it.
Fly-Blow Yeah, spend it, of course. But what on?
Bad Grub Ooh... (*He thinks*) Stuff.
Fly-Blow What sort of stuff?
Bad Grub You know ... stuff, from a shop. (*He holds out his arms*) This sort of stuff. (*He holds his arms another way*) And this sort of stuff. And small stuff too, but good quality.
Fly-Blow Yeah, I'm going to get some of that stuff an' all.
Bad Grub That's not fair! You get your own stuff.
Fly-Blow (*beginning to stand*) All right I will. An' my stuff'll be better than your stuff, you'll see.
Bad Grub (*beginning to stand*) Yeah? Well when I've bought all my stuff there won't be any stuff left for you, so there.
Fly-Blow (*standing*) Then I'll smash all your stuff so you won't have any stuff either.
Bad Grub (*standing*) Yeah?
Fly-Blow Yeah.

They are about to come to blows when Bruiser enters pulling the cage with Rosie in. Hanging from the cart are the instruments that the Bad Apples stole from Mr Crispin SCENE 1

The quarrel is forgotten

Bruiser (*puffed out*) Bad Grub, why do I have to be the one to pull this? It's heavy.
Bad Grub We'll all take a turn, Bruiser, but as you found her you have the honour of going first.
Bruiser Then whose turn is it next?

Fly-Blow (*grinning*) No-one's. Bad Grub says we're going to stay here and wait for the Pieman. (*He calls*) Piema—an. Mr Piema—an.

Bad Grub joins in with the calling. Bruiser puzzles over what's just occurred

Rosie Please don't hand me over to the Pieman. You know what he'll do with me, don't you?
Bad Apples (*matter of fact*) Put you in a pie.
Rosie I don't understand how you can do this to another apple, one of your own kind. It can't be because you hate me, you hardly know me.
Bad Grub Nah, of course we don't *hate* you, do we lads?

Bruiser and Fly-Blow shake their heads

This is strictly business. We're just doing our job.
Bruiser And if we don't deliver you to the Pieman we get put in the pie instead.

Bad grub gives Bruiser a kick

Rosie Then we should try to stop him. If you'll set me free I'll join your gang and we can fight the Pieman and his wickedness together. We could get other apples to help us and ——
Bad Grub You — join us? I don't think so.
Rosie Why not?

Bad Grub gives a knowing wink to his pals

Bad Grub Because …

Song No.3: The Bad Apple Rap

During the introduction the Bad Apples take their instruments and play or dance to the music

Bad Apples   (*singing*) We're the bad apples, the worst of the crop.
                        We're mean guys and streetwise, hard apples of rock.
                        We won't go to school and we don't clean our shoes.
                        We push to the front when we're standing in queues.
                        Bad Apples.
                        Bad Apples.
Rosie   Please, Mr Bad Grub, give me a chance.
                        I'll learn to be rotten, you could teach me to dance.

	Whatever you do I'll be there to pitch in
	If you won't let me end up in the Pieman's kitchen.
Bad Apples	Cooking apple.
	Cooking apple.
Bad Grub	Now listen here, Rosie, 'cos I'm telling you
	You're the wrong sort of apple to mix with this crew.
	You're sweet and you're clean,
	You say "Please", you say "Thanks".
Bad Apples	We get into bovver
	You get up to pranks.
	Goody Apple, yerrch!
	Goody Apple.

There is a guitar solo to which Bad Grub mimes and Fly-Blow and Bruiser dance

During the following verse Polly Pippin comes out of hiding and lets Rosie out of the cage. Then, together, they get hold of Bruiser and put him in the cart in place of Rosie

Rosie and Polly run off stage

We hear the Pieman's ominous footsteps

> (*Singing*) Here comes the Pieman and he's ready to cook
> With his spoon and his bowl and his recipe book.
> He'll chop you in pieces and mix you with spice.
> Sauté you! *Flambé* you! You're gonna taste nice.
> As a mover, a groover you're really a flop.
> But in a pie, my oh my, top of the pops!
> A big hit now,
> A prize-winner.
> A big hit now,
> A prize-winner.
> Bad apples!
> Bad apples!
> Bad apples!

The Pieman enters

Pieman Stop it! Stop this racket at once. It's enough to turn pie crust soggy.

Bad Grub and Fly-Blow stop singing and dancing

You called?

Bad Grub Yes, Mr Pieman, sir. I think you're going to be pleased with us. Very pleased indeed.

Pieman I'd better be.

Bad Grub (*proudly*) We've got Rosie. You know, that apple you told us to look for. Remember?

Pieman Of course I remember. Well, where is she?

Bad Grub (*glancing nervously at Fly-Blow*) All in good time, Guv, all in good time. First there's the little matter regarding our fee.

Pieman Fee? What fee?

Bad Grub "Do a good job and you'll get your reward," were, I think, your exact words at the time.

Pieman Were they indeed? Now that I don't remember, it was all so long ago.

Bad Grub stands his ground

All right, all right, perhaps I did mention it. But only if the goods are in tip-top condition; no bruises, no blemishes and crisp as the day that she was picked. Keep your part of the bargain and I'll keep mine.

Bad Grub Fair enough. She's in there. (*Without looking he throws open the cage door*)

Pieman Are you trying to trick me?

Bad Grub No, Guv, why would we do that?

Pieman Then what, pray tell me, is that manky, fly-blown, canker-ridden piece of putrefaction doing in there.

Bad Grub looks in and is stunned to see Bruiser. Bad Grub and Fly-Blow pull Bruiser out of the cart

Fly-Blow How did you end up in there?

Bruiser I was pushed in. There was about five of them. I tried to fight 'em off but they got the better of me.

Bad Grub (*to Bruiser*) Grrr! (*To the Pieman*) She must've got away, Guv. Apparently she had a whole gang of 'em to help her.

Pieman You'll need a whole gang to help you if you don't get her back, and quick! My patience is running out.

The Pieman exits

Bad Grub Right! We'd better start looking — again.

Bruiser Er — Bad Grub, now Rosie's gone can I ride for a bit?

Bad Grub }
Fly-Blow } (*together*) No!!!

Bruiser Sorry.

The Bad Apples are about to exit when the Pieman re-enters

Pieman Oh, Bad Grub.
Bad Grub Yes, Mr Pieman.
Pieman Don't call me Guv.
Bad Grub Tch! Did I call you Guv, Guv? Can't think how that happened.
Pieman And don't call me Guv Guv either.
Bad Grub No! Course not! Wouldn't dream of calling you Guv Guv, Guv.
Pieman (*through clenched teeth*) Bad Grub! Don't call me Guv, or Guv Guv,
    or Guv Guv Guv. Get it?
Bad Grub Yes, Tosh.

The Pieman snarls and exits

*Rumbles of thunder are heard. Music underscore (**No.3a.**) continues*

The Bad Apples quickly exit in the opposite direction

SCENE 6

ANOTHER PART OF THE FOREST

It is getting dark

*Unseen as yet, set US is a pair of gates. Hanging over them, is an unlit practical
light. There is a chain leading to a bell and there is a brass plate, which reads,
" The Amelia Crabapple Home for Orphaned Apples"*

Rosie and Polly enter, breathless from their escape

Rosie That was a really brave thing you did back there, risking your own life
    to save mine.
Polly That's all right. I could see you was in a spot of bother so I thought I'd
    help out.
Rosie Just when I was beginning to think there wasn't a good apple left in
    the whole of Appledom. I'm Rosie, by the way. (*She extends a hand to
    Polly*)
Polly Polly. Polly Pippin.
Rosie Well I'm jolly glad to have met you, Polly. (*She pauses*) Gosh it's dark.
    Do you know where we are?
Polly (*looking around*) I'm not sure. I've never been in this part of the forest
    before.

Rosie I guess that means we're lost. What do we do now?

A Light appears US

Look! There's a light over there. D'you see it? It could be a house, shall we
find out?

Rosie and Polly move US *to investigate*

*As they approach the light it gets brighter, revealing the gates, the brass plate
and the bell chain*

(*Reading out*) "The Amelia Crabapple home for orphaned apples."
Polly I'm an orphan.
Rosie So am I — sort of. I got separated from my parents when I was a baby,
but I hope to find them again one day. This Amelia Crabapple must be
awfully nice if she's willing to share her home with a lot of orphans. I'm
sure we'll be safe here.
Polly I don't know. Somehow it doesn't look very — welcoming to me.
Rosie Oh you mustn't go by appearances. Never judge an apple by its skin,
Granny used to say — she's the one who brought me up — and she was
a good example. Her house wasn't exactly welcoming, but she was the
warmest, kindest, most welcoming apple you could wish to … (*She
becomes tearful*)
Polly Don't cry, Rosie.
Rosie I'm all right, just tired and very hungry. Come on, what d'you say, shall
we ring the bell? We don't have to stay long, only until the Bad Apples are
far enough away.
Polly All right, if you think so.

Rosie pulls the bell chain

*The bell rings and the gates swing open as though someone has been waiting
for them*

A figure appears. It is Amelia Crabapple

Amelia Come inside, little applekins, come inside. Life can be so hard for
poor little orphaned apples like you. But a good night's sleep and things
will seem different in the morning. (*To the audience*) Quite different.

*Rosie and Polly are too tired to resist as Amelia sweeps them through the
gates which clang ominously shut behind them*

*Music underscore (**No.3b.**) continues*

Black-out

SCENE 7

INSIDE THE ORPHANAGE, THE FOLLOWING DAY

The Orphanage doubles as a laundry and there should be a wash tub, a mangle, a line with washing pegged out, perhaps an ironing table with a flat iron. There is a comfortable chair for Amelia. The Orphange gates remain visible on one side of the stage

The scene opens in black-out

Amelia Come along you orphans, it's getting up time!!!

Lights come up on the interior of the Orphanage

> *The orphans enter, dragging their feet and yawning. They are a gloomy looking lot in their dull smocks. Amelia enters with them carrying two grey smocks for Rosie and Polly. We see Amelia properly for the first time. She is a greedy, vain and silly apple with a spiteful streak. She can be more childish than the young apples in her care*

The children begin to wash, iron and mangle

> *Polly and Rosie enter*

Amelia Good morning, girls. I trust you slept well.
Rosie Mm, not bad thank you, although the bed was rather lumpy.
Amelia How very unpleasant for you. I'll have to see what I can do about that.
Rosie That's very kind, but you shouldn't bother. We won't be staying long. Um ... where do we have breakfast?
Amelia Now where would you like to have it, in the morning room, or the garden, or perhaps you'd like to pop back into bed and have me bring it to you there, on a tray?
Rosie Well, we — er ...
Amelia You see here it's not so much a question of where you get fed as when you get fed. And that's after you've done some work. Bessie! Show these two what to do. And put on these. (*She thrusts the two smocks at Rosie and Polly*)

Bessie takes the bewildered pair and puts them to work

Rosie (*looking around*) This isn't an orphanage, it's a workhouse. It's not right to treat young apples like this. When we get out of here I shall tell Granny Smith. She'll put a stop to it.

Bessie eavesdrops the conversation

Bessie You won't get out of here until you're due. Miss Amelia won't let you.
Rosie I'm not going to be kept here against my will. I shall run away if I have to.
Bessie You'll have to see Bob about that. Bob!

Bessie calls to a bespectacled boy, who joins them

This one here says she wants to escape.
Bob Does she? All escape plans have to be submitted in triplicate to the escape committee.
Rosie Who's that?
Bob Me.
Polly What for?
Bob You can't have orphans escaping just when they feel like it.
Rosie Why not?

Bob begins to feel dizzy from the interrogation

During the following a small apple in a large fake beard, who is trying to escape, enters

Bob B—b—because it has to be properly organized. You need a plan, maps, disguises, forged papers. (*He gets out a notebook*) If you'd like to put in your application now I'll see what I can do, but I must warn you there's a long waiting list.
Polly (*nudging Rosie*) Look.

Polly draws Rosie's attention to the small apple in the large fake beard. He saunters past Amelia who appears not to notice him, then she puts out a hand and pulls down the beard

Amelia Tommy?
Tommy (*sighing*) Yes, Miss Amelia.
Amelia Not bad, but not good enough. Get back to work.

The dejected apple returns to work

An orphan enters disguised as laundry — feet through the bottom of a laundry basket, dirty washing on top. This basket is carried on by two more orphans

Amelia lifts up the washing exposing the escape

Amelia Running an orphanage can be fun. Don't know about you, but I've worked up quite an appetite. Breakfast time!

A couple of orphans scurry off and return with a tray of bowls of food and spoons which are then handed out to the others. Another brings a plate of delicious cakes for Amelia

Amelia takes the cakes but as she moves one drops to the floor. A boy stoops to pick it up. Amelia smiles at him, but just as he is about to take a bite she swipes it from him

   Mine. (*She sits and eats*)

The orphans take their bowls of food and eat

Rosie At least she's not going to starve us, there's plenty here. (*She takes a mouthful*) Ugh, it's awful.
Polly Not very nice is it?
Rosie I'm sorry I got you into this mess, Polly. You didn't want to come in here, I could tell, but I thought I knew best. I promise I'll get us out of here, one way or another.
Amelia Measuring time! Line up now, nice and straight.

The bigger orphans jump up and form a line. Bessie indicates that Rosie and Polly should do the same. They stand at the end of the line next to Bob. Amelia takes a tape measure from her pocket and measures each apple around its girth. She also tests their plumpness by pinching and squeezing them, sometimes rather hard

Polly What's going on?
Bob She's measuring us for our uniforms.
Rosie I don't understand.
Bob When we grow too big to stay down here we're sent 'upstairs' where there's a brand new uniform waiting for us, especially made.
Amelia (*to a girl apple*) You're no bigger than you were last time. (*She looks into the girl's bowl*) Aha! You've not been eating all your rations. Finish that up at once.

The girl obeys, pulling a face

Polly Is it better up there than down here?
Bob Much better. Once an orphan goes upstairs they never come down here again, not even for a visit.

Rosie and Polly look at each other with concern. Amelia measures Bob

Amelia Well, Bob, I think by tomorrow you'll be ready to go "upstairs".
Bob I will?! Oh thank you, Miss Amelia.
Amelia I bet you can't wait to get into your new uniform.

Amelia measures Rosie and Polly

Professor Crispin arrives. He was formerly 'Mr Crispin', who should have played at the party in Scene 1 *and now he has graduated and become a teacher. He carries a music briefcase and wears a college scarf. He removes his scarf and puts down his case*

You two need plumping up. Double rations from now on. I see the Professor has arrived. School time.

There is much activity as the breakfast things are cleared away and some stools or forms are brought on to make a schoolroom. Amelia picks up her plate of cakes and moves to the Professor

Good morning, Professor Crispin.
Crispin Good morning, Miss Amelia. Yes, I'd love a honeycake. How clever of you to guess that I hadn't had any breakfast. (*He helps himself to several cakes*).
Amelia (*indignant*) Well of all the … (*She turns away, hugging the plate*)

While Amelia's back is turned, Professor Crispin throws the cakes he has taken to some of the orphans. Amelia sits in her chair and nurses her plate of cakes

Crispin Good morning class.
Class Good morning Professor Crispin.
Crispin I see we have two new pupils today. Would you like to tell me your names?
Polly Polly.
Rosie Rosie.
Crispin (*thoughtfully*) Rosie? Rosie? Have we met before? You seem familiar.

Rosie I don't think so.

Crispin Perhaps not then. I think we'll start with arithmetic. If I have twelve honey cakes and I give one to Rosie, two to Bessie and three to Bob, how many will I have left?

Amelia Professor, I'll thank you not to go giving my orphans ideas. Honeycakes indeed. Where would I find the money to feed them honey cakes? Why I can barely make ends meet as it is. (*She stuffs a cake into her mouth*)

Crispin I'm sorry. It doesn't have to be honey cakes, it can be anything you like, ribbons, buttons, biscuits … er, no … not biscuits.

Amelia I should think not.

Crispin I'm only trying to teach them something they'll find useful when they finally leave here.

Amelia (*aside*) They won't have much use for counting honey cakes where they're going.

Crispin I beg your pardon.

Amelia (*feigning emotion*) I said, it always makes me sad when I think of them going. I know, why don't you get them to sing The Happy Apple song? You know how it cheers me up.

All the orphans groan

Crispin (*wearily*) Very well.

The Bad Apples enter and they ring the gate bell

Amelia Shan't be a tick. (*She rises and crosses to the gates*) Don't start without me.

The Professor Crispin opens his music case and searches through it. The orphans chat quietly and play as youngster do when the adults aren't looking. Amelia opens the gates and, without even looking to see who is there, starts her well practised speech

Come inside, little applekins, come in — (*She spots Bad Grub and company*). Ugh, no! Shoo, shoo! Get away you filthy disgusting creatures. I take in orphans not garbage.

Bad Grub Hey, wait a minute. We're not garbage, we're businessmen and we're here on … er … business.

Amelia What sort of business?

Bad Grub We're looking for an apple called Rosie.

Amelia and the Bad Apples freeze while our attention goes back to the classroom. Professor Crispin rummages through his music case looking for some song sheets

Crispin Dear me, I don't seem to have the song sheets. Rosie, would you go and ask Miss Amelia for the key to the music cupboard?
Rosie Yes, sir. (*She crosses towards Amelia*)

Amelia and the Bad Apples come back to life as Rosie crosses to them. Rosie is horrified to find her talking to the Bad Apples. She hides herself and listens

Amelia Rosie? Rosie? I've got several Rosies in here. Any one of them might be yours, or none of them. How would I know?
Fly-Blow (*trying to get a foot in the gates*) If you'd let us come in we could see for ourselves.

Amelia pushes Fly-Blow back

Amelia Oh no, you're not coming in here. (*Pause*) What do you want her for anyway?
Bruiser For the Pieman.

Bad Grub gives Bruiser a kick

Amelia (*feigning shock*) You want me to let you have one of my sweet little orphans so you can give her to someone who'll chop her up and put her in a pie? What kind of an apple d'you think I am? (*Pause*) How much is he paying you for this?
Bad Grub (*with shame*) Fifty p.
Amelia Fifty p!? Fifty p!? Why, he pays me twice as much as that. And I don't deal in ones, in Rosies, I sell 'em to him in dozens. Dozens and dozens. Now be off with you, you are nothing but a lot of amateurs. I am a professional.

She slams the gate leaving the Bad Apples stunned. She passes Rosie and stops to preen herself before moving on to the classroom

Bad Grub Would you believe it, this orphanage is nothing but a front.
Bruiser No, Bad Grub, it's got a back too. I saw it down the side.
Bad Grub No, stupid, a front. A cover for a diabolical scheme she's operating. See, she lures in poor little innocent orphans who've nowhere else to go, and then she turns them over to the Pieman.
Bruiser (*tearfully*) Oh, Bad Grub, that's terrible.
Bad Grub Yeah — wish I'd thought of it.
Fly-Blow We might as well go. There's no point us hanging round here. If Rosie's in there the Pieman's going to get her — one way or another.

Bad Grub Yeah, but one way we don't get our money and I'm blowed if I've
   come all this way for nothing.
Fly-Blow You got a plan, BG?
Bad Grub Not yet, Fly-Blow, but if we stay here long enough I'm bound to
   come up with something.

*The Bad Apples settle down to wait and, during the scene, fall asleep. Our
attention goes back to the classroom where the Professor finds the song
sheets in his briefcase and hands them out. Rosie comes out of hiding and
joins the class*

Crispin Ah, Rosie, I had the song sheets all along. Here's one for you.
Amelia I'm looking forward to this.

The class get into their positions ready to sing. Rosie sidles up to Polly

Rosie Oh, Polly, we're in terrible, terrible danger. We've got to get out of
   here — all of us. (*She puts a hand to Polly's face and whispers in her ear*)

An expression of horror appears on Polly's face

Polly What are we going to do?

*The Professor takes out a small harmonica and a baton from his briefcase.
He blows a note on the harmonica. The orphans all hum the note. The
Professor raises his baton*

Rosie (*slightly hysterical*) Do?! Do?! What else can we do? We sing.

The less-than-happy orphans sing

Song No.4: The Happy Apple Song

Orphans   Don't be a sour face when you can wear a grin,
                    Be a Happy Apple and you'll win.
                    If Dame Fortune ignores you or kicks you in the shin
                    Be a Happy Apple and you'll win.

                    And you'll win. (*Echo*) And you'll win.
                    Yes you'll win.
                    Though life is tough and getting tougher
                    The more you smile the less you'll suffer.
                    Be a Happy Apple and you'll win.

When your porridge is lumpy and your custard has a skin,
Be a Happy Apple and you'll win.
Or the roof's badly leaking and rain is pouring in,
Be a Happy Apple and you'll win.

Oh you'll win
yes you'll win
An apple's life is not all honey,
Just wear a smile and make it sunny.
Be a Happy Apple and you'll win.

Be a Happy Apple, though life can be a battle.
Be a Happy Apple, one day you'll win the raffle.

Instrumental

Though the sun has got his hat off
And the clouds are gathering,
Be a Happy Apple and you'll win.
When you've no-one to turn to and danger's closing in,
Be a Happy Apple and you'll win.

And you'll win.
Oh you'll win
When you've got that unloved feeling
A smile can make you more appealing.
Be a Happy Apple and you'll win.

At the end of the song the orphans return to their schoolwork

Amelia exits

Heads down, the class beaver away. A clock strikes two and the Orphans look up

Crispin Well done, you've worked hard today. Don't forget to do the sums I set for homework. (*He prepares to leave*) I'll see you all tomorrow.

Bob puts up his hand

Amelia enters, with a fresh plate of honeycakes

Bob Please, Sir, you won't see me tomorrow. (*He speaks with pride*) Miss Amelia says I'm ready to go *upstairs*.

Crispin Well done, Bob. Jolly good, jolly good. Do your best there, won't you? Don't let us down.

Amelia He won't, Professor. Once they get *upstairs* my little orphans never let me down. They're always at their best.

Professor Crispin moves towards the gate

Polly Why don't we tell Professor Crispin what's going on here, Rosie, quickly, before he goes?

Rosie But he could be in league with Miss Amelia. Granny said the Pieman turns good apples into bad apples so you never know who to trust.

Professor Crispin exits

Polly watches Professor Crispin go, somewhat wistfully

Polly He looks … really kind.

Amelia Right, you orphans, back to work while I have a tiny snack and my afternoon snooze.

Amelia sits, gobbles down a couple of cakes and nods off. Some of the orphans make towards the exit in order to fetch the laundry equipment. Rosie   calls the orphans back and beckons to the others to gather round

Rosie (*with one eye on Amelia*) I've something important to tell you. This is not a good place to be in, you must get out of here as soon as possible.

Bessie What does she mean "it's not a good place"? It's not that bad, we get three meals a day.

Rosie takes a deep breath as she prepares to tell them the truth

Rosie If you stay here you will all be sold to the Pieman.

Young Apple Waah! I don't want to be sold to the Pieman, I don't like him. And I don't like her, she's scaring me.

Bessie (*comforting the young apple*) She's scaring us all. You've no business saying things like that, you're just making trouble.

Bob She's been a troublemaker ever since she got here, trying to pinch my job as escape committee. I'm going to tell Miss Amelia.

Polly No! You mustn't do that. Please listen to Rosie, she's telling the truth.

The orphans seem to believe Polly and quieten down

Rosie You know when Miss Amelia measures you to see if you're ready to go *upstairs*?

The orphans nod

I don't think she's measuring you for some new clothes, I think she's measuring you to see if you'll fit in a pie dish. *Upstairs* is just another name for the Pieman's larder.

Everyone gasps

Orphan (*slowly*) Is that why the orphans who go *upstairs* are never seen again?

Rosie nods

Bob Does that mean I won't get a nice new uniform?
Polly No, Bob. Not unless you call a piecrust a uniform.
Bob (*slowly the penny drops*) But I'm supposed to go upstairs tomorrow. Ooooooh!!! I don't like this, I've got to get out of here.

The orphans begin to panic. Amelia snores, but remains asleep

Polly Shush! That's what Rosie's been trying to tell you. We've all got to get out of here.
Bessie (*tearfully*) But how? You saw how good she is at catching us.
Rosie I know, I know. We'll just have to find a way that's not been tried before. Just let me think.

There is complete hush while Rosie thinks, punctuated only by Amelia's snores. Rosie looks at her

Have you ever tried escaping while she's asleep?

Everyone shakes their heads

That's it then. One by one we'll tip-toe past Miss Amelia. When you're through the gates, split up and run as fast as you can. And be on the look-out for the Pieman. Polly, you go first and open the gates.

*Music underscore (**No.4a**) continues*

While Rosie organizes the orphans, Polly runs to the gates, sees the Bad Apples, who are asleep, and returns to Rosie

Polly The Bad Apples are still out there, but I think they're asleep too.

Rosie I'd forgotten about them. We'll have to tip-toe past them as well.

Polly goes back to open the gates. The orphans start to tip-toe past Amelia. Polly helps them through the gates

Throughout the scene, the orphans exit off stage slowly

As Bob passes Amelia he sneaks a honeycake off her plate. Amelia stirs

Amelia (*sleepily*) Who's that stealing my honeycakes. (*She opens an eye and sees what is happening*) Whaaaaat!!!!
Rosie Run, Bob, run!

Bob runs towards the gate and exits. Rosie bravely grabs the plate of cakes and throws them in Amelia's face. Then, she helps the remaining orphans to escape before she too exits

Amelia staggers around the stage, looking for an alarm button

Amelia Where's the alarm? Where's the alarm? Somebody do something, the orphans are getting away.

She locates the alarm bell and presses it. Pandemonium breaks out. A siren sounds, a searchlight strafes the stage and audience

The Bad Apples wake up from all the noise. Amelia rushes to the gates

Stop them! Stop them I say!
Bad Grub What is it? What's going on?
Amelia That — that Rosie, she's helped all my orphans to escape. I want them back. I want her back. And when I get her back she'll pay for what she's done. I'll make her suffer. Follow that apple!

Still half asleep, the Bad Apples are too confused to argue. They take up the chase, possibly through the audience

The CURTAIN *falls*

II. Entr'acte

ACT TWO

Scene 1

A House Not Far From The Orphanage

A small cottage in a clearing with some bushes

In the distance we hear the sound of the chase — the siren, shouting and screaming. As the scene begins the siren fades away

Rosie and Polly enter, out of breath. Rosie is wet and bedraggled

Polly Rosie, are you all right?
Rosie Yes, I think so, just rather wet. It was stupid of me to go and fall in that stream. Brr, it's chilly.
Polly Why don't we knock on that door and ask if we can come in and dry off?
Rosie No, Polly. We don't know who lives there and they might send us straight back to the orphanage.

They hear a noise

Shush! I think someone's coming. Hide!

Polly and Rosie hide behind the bushes

Professor Crispin enters carrying a bag of shopping. He goes to the cottage door and takes out his key

Rosie shivers which makes the bushes shake

Crispin (*alarmed*) Who's there? (*He pauses*) Answer me now. I know someone's there.

Rosie sneezes

(*He reaches into his shopping bag and takes out a bread stick, which he brandishes*) I warn you that I am armed and if there's any unpleasantness

I shall not hesitate to defend myself. Aha! I see you. (*He points the bread at the bush behind which Polly is hiding*) Come on now, come out and show yourself. No use trying to hide.

Polly stands up and steps out from behind the bushes

Polly? What are you doing here? Are you lost? (*Taking a step towards her*) Let me take you back to the orphanage, Miss Amelia will be worried about you.

Rosie leaps out in front of the surprised Professor and grabs the bread stick

Rosie Oh no you don't, Professor Crispin. You're not taking her back to that dreadful place — nor me either.

Crispin Rosie?! You too? What's this all about?

Rosie About? I'll tell you what it's about. It's about freedom. It's about poor little orphaned apples being free of the fear of being turned into pie filling by the likes of you and that Amelia Crabapple.

Crispin What in Appledom are you talking about? (*To Polly*) Is she ill?

Rosie shivers

My dear girl, you are ill — you're shivering. (*Taking a step towards Rosie*) Come inside and get warm.

Rosie (*brandishing the bread stick*) One step nearer and I too shall not hesitate to defend myself.

Crispin Rosie, do you know what that is you are holding?

Rosie No.

Crispin It's a loaf of honeybread.

Rosie Oh!

Professor Crispin takes the bread stick from her

What are you going to do?

Crispin Well, I'm going to take this inside and have it sliced and toasted with a cup of honey tea. Care to join me?

Professor Crispin unlocks the door and holds it open

Polly looks at Rosie, shrugs and goes in. Rosie follows, if somewhat uncertainly. Professor Crispin goes in and shuts the door

SCENE 2

INSIDE CRISPIN'S HOUSE

The inside of Professor Crispin's house is cosy, albeit shabby and rather untidy. In amongst the clutter there is an old make-up box, the type that is used for amateur dramatics. There is a screen in one corner and a clothes chest and cupboard. There is a mantelpiece with a map, various cards, and objects. There is a table set for tea

Crispin, Polly and Rosie sit round the table finishing their tea. Rosie is wrapped in a blanket

Rosie Then Polly opened the gates ——
Polly — and Rosie got the orphans to tip-toe past Miss Amelia ——
Rosie — but she woke up and ——
Polly — raised the alarm, so we ran as fast as we could.
Rosie Now they are all after me, the Pieman, Miss Amelia, the Bad Apples...
Crispin I could see Miss Amelia had her faults, but I never suspected her of being downright evil. And to think it was all going on under my very nose. The appleskins I might have saved if I hadn't been so blind. (*He puts his head in his hands*) I shall never forgive myself.
Polly No use feeling sorry for yourself, Professor. It won't undo what's been done.
Crispin No, Polly, you're right, it won't. But I must do something to make up for my stupidity. (*He thinks hard*) I shall devote the rest of my life to protecting any orphaned apple who comes knocking at my door.
Polly That's the spirit.
Rosie You were right, Polly, when you said he looked kind.

Polly blushes. Professor Crispin looks flustered, but pleased

Crispin Did she say that?
Rosie (*shivering*) Yes ... she's a much b...b...better judge of ch...ch...character than me.
Polly You ought to get out of those wet clothes, Rosie.
Crispin (*jumping up*) I'll get you something of mine to wear while they're drying.

Professor Crispin takes some clothes from the chest and gives them to Rosie. He indicates that she can change behind the screen

Will you two do me the honour of being the first to accept my offer of protection?

Polly Thanks, but Rosie wants to get back to her Granny to let her know that she's safe. I said I'd go with her.

Crispin What a shame! I was so enjoying your delightful company — that is, the company of you both, I mean.

Rosie tosses her wet dress over the screen and her locket falls to the floor. Professor Crispin picks it up and examines it

Rosie, is this your locket?

Rosie Yes, why?

Crispin I think I know these apples.

Rosie pops ups and looks over or around the screen

Rosie What?

Crispin The pictures are rather faded, but I believe they're of my dearest friends Rufus and Rhoda Russet.

Rosie hurries out from behind the screen. She is wrapped in the blanket

Rosie And I believe they're of my dear parents! —So I must be ——

Crispin So you must be — Rosie Russet! I should have seen the family likeness the minute I set eyes on you, but then I'm not the most observant apple, am I?

Rosie How was I separated from them, do you know?

Crispin Of course, I was there when it happened. It was at the party after you'd been picked, the Pieman wanted to take you to … to … put in a pie. Your mother tried to put you back on the tree, she knew he couldn't touch you there, but that made him angry and so he blew you away.

Rosie Straight into Granny Smith … thank goodness.

Crispin For a while I helped your parents look for you, but then I had to go back to college.

Rosie So they did look for me! I was sure they would.

Crispin Still are looking. (*He takes a card from the mantelpiece and gives it to Rosie*) I had a card from them just yesterday. Here.

Rosie takes the card

Rosie (*reading, emotionally*) "Dear Crispin, no news of our Rosie here in Bramleyville. The Pieman's cursed breath must have carried her further than we thought. Catching the next strong wind that blows this way to continue our search for her in foreign parts. As long as we have the strength we will keep looking for our dear daughter. Yours, Rufus and Rhoda Russet." I must get to them before they leave. How far is it to Bramleyville?

Crispin About a day's journey. Though it is not an easy one. There are many dangers.

Polly Especially if those Bad Apples and Miss Amelia are still after you.

Crispin Why not stay here and write to your parents? A letter should reach Bramleyville in time.

Rosie But if it didn't then I'd have missed my best, perhaps my only chance of ever finding them. I must go to Bramleyville, now. Do you have a map, Professor?

Crispin I think so. It's here somewhere I'm sure. (*He searches for the map and finds it*) I have it! (*He spreads the map out on top of the tea things*) First you must go through Hallowe'en Wood. Whatever you do, don't fall asleep in that place. Keep on this path until you come to the crossroads then follow the sign that points to Bramleyville. Take care not to end up in the Maggot Marshes, many an apple has been known to perish in that unwholesome place.

Rosie leans over to look at the map and lets the blanket drop, revealing herself in Crispin's clothes

Polly Rosie! You look just like a boy apple.

Crispin Remarkably like my young brother.

Crispin }
Polly } (*together*) Are you thinking what I'm thinking?

Polly That the Bad Apples won't be looking for a boy?

Crispin If we could make you look a bit older that would help. (*He fetches an old make-up box*) Used to do a spot of amateur theatricals at one time. (*He gets a moustache on some elastic, puts it over Rosie's head and fits it under her nose*) How's that?

Polly nods her approval

I'll get some food for your journey.

Crispin exits

Polly Let me come with you. It'll be safer with two.

Rosie (*taking off her mask*) No, Polly, I should do this on my own. Besides, Professor Crispin will need you here. He'll have his hands full when all those runaway orphans come knocking at his door.

They laugh

But, thank you. Thanks for everything. I wouldn't be here now if it wasn't for you.

During the following song Rosie and Polly and move DS. *A spot light comes up on Rosie and Polly. The next scene is set up behind them*

Song No. 5: A Friend Like You

Rosie	It's nice to know I've got a friend like you, Polly. You're good at all the things that I can't do. And your instincts are a must When knowing who to trust. It's nice to know I've got a friend like you.
Polly	It's nice to know I've got a friend like you, Rosie. You're honest, fair and decent through and through. And you're not afraid to fight, To stand up for what's right. It's nice to know I've got a friend like you.
Both	Now it's time for us to say adieu And our sep'rate paths we must pursue. If those paths don't cross again Our friendship will remain, A friendship that will last a lifetime through.
Rosie	I'll always know I've got a friend like you.
Polly	Always know I've got a friend like you.
Rosie	Nice to know I've ——
Both	Got a friend like you.

Professor Crispin enters with a bag of food, the map and a cap, and gives them to Rosie

Rosie Look after Polly for me won't you, Professor?

Polly Look after me, why it's him that wants looking after! When I was living wild, in the forest, I kept it tidier than his house.

Rosie Goodbye, Polly.

Polly 'Bye, Rosie.

They hug

Rosie Goodbye, Professor.

Crispin Goodbye, Rosie, and good luck.

They shake hands

Rosie puts on the cap and her moustache, and exits, with her bag of food and map in satchel

Remember — don't sleep in Hallowe'en Wood tonight!

Polly Well, Professor, I think it's time we made a start on those mucky tea things.

Crispin You know, Polly, I'd really rather like it if you'd call me Crispin.

Polly and Professor Crispin exit

*Music underscore (**No.5a.**) continues*

Black-out

SCENE 3

HALLOWE'EN WOOD

Hallowe'en wood

It is dusk, the time when Hallowe'en Wood is at its spookiest. Throughout the following scene sudden bursts of strange noises add to the eerie atmosphere

The Bad Apples enter, pulling the cage/cart with Amelia inside. She still cradles her bag of cakes in her arms

Amelia Can't you go any faster, we'll never catch up with that Rosie at this rate?

Bruiser Here, Bad Grub, do we have to go any further? It's getting dark and it's scary round here.

Amelia Great big apple like you scared of the dark? Oh diddums.

Fly-Blow Well I'm with Bruiser, BG. Not that I'm scared mind you, just tired of pulling this thing. Her and her bag of cakes weigh a ton.

Amelia I need sustenance for the journey.

Bad Grub Yeah, well so do we, so hand 'em out.

Amelia But they're mine.

Bad Grub Look here, if *you* don't share 'em out *we* won't take you any further and you'll have to stay here on your own.

Amelia Oh, very well. (*She climbs out of the cart and then, rather grudgingly, hands out the cakes*) That's — one for you and two for me — and one for you and four for me — and I'll take one back and you give that to him …

The Bad Apples are left with only one cake between them

Bad Grub Right! Now I suggest that we stay here for the night, get some rest and go after Rosie in the morning. One of us will have to stand guard though … er … Bruiser, you take first watch.

Amelia and Fly-Blow sit and make themselves comfortable

Bruiser But, Bad Grub, that means that I'll be awake, on my own, while you're all asleep. If something scary's going to happen — I want to be asleep too.

Bad Grub We'll all take our turn, Bruiser, but you have to go first. Here's what you do. You march up and down and if anyone comes you say, "Halt! Who goes there, friend or foe?" If they say "friend" you say, "Advance friend and be recognized," and if they look all right, you let them pass.

Bruiser What if they don't look all right?

Fly-Blow You wake us up and we — sort 'em out.

Bad Grub Got that? (*He sits down*)

Bruiser I think so. (*He marches up and down chanting very loudly*) Who goes there — friend or foe? Who goes there — friend or foe? Who goes there …

Amelia (*trying to sleep*) *Sotto voce*, if you don't mind.

Bruiser What?

Bad Grub ⎫
Fly-Blow ⎭ (*together*) Quietly!

Bruiser tip-toes up and down in an exaggerated manner while whispering "Who goes there etc". Amelia, Bad Grub and Fly-Blow fall asleep

As it grows dark, the wood comes to life with creepy noises

Bruiser walks backwards as though trying to escape the noises

Rosie enters backwards, carrying a satchel or a rucksack. She is also scared of the noises. She and Bruiser bump, gasp and turn around to face each other as they did in Act I Scene 4

Bruiser You scared me.

Rosie (*speaking in her normal voice, forgetting that she is dressed as a boy*) You scared me — I mean — (*speaking in a deeper voice*) you scared me too.

Bruiser Now what was I supposed to say … Oh yeah. Halt, who goes there, Fred or Flo?

Rosie Fred or Flo — ? But I'm neither.

Bruiser You've got to be one or the other or I won't know what to do and then I'll have to wake Bad Grub and ask him and he'll be ever so cross and ——

Rosie No, no, no, don't do that! All right — I'll be Fred.

Bruiser (*pleased with himself*) Advance Fred and be recognized.

Rosie takes a cautious step towards Bruiser

Hey! I recognize you!

Rosie (*coughing and trying to hide her face*) I don't think you do, I've never been in this neck of the woods before. Look, I must be getting along. There's someone I'm supposed to meet. (*She shakes Bruiser's hand*). It's been a pleasure knowing you, Bruiser. I …(*She gasps, realizing what a gaffe she's made*)

Bruiser keeps hold of Rosie's hand

Bruiser How do you know my name?

Rosie Well, you … er …look like an apple who'd be called Bruiser.

Rosie gives Bruiser a friendly punch. He puffs out his chest thinking that Fred sees him as a tough apple. He finally releases Rosie's hand

Bruiser S'pose I do. Now look here, Fred … (*Putting a friendly arm round Rosie*) … you don't want to be wandering around these woods all alone.

Rosie I don't?

Bruiser No. It's scary and you don't know what you might bump into.

There is a sudden burst of spooky and strange noises

Why don't you stay here with us? You'll be quite safe with me standing guard.

Rosie Awfully decent of you, but I should be getting along …

Another burst of spooky noises frightens Rosie

Bruiser That's settled then. (*He propels Rosie to a sleeping place*) You make yourself comfy and don't worry about a thing.

Rosie edges away from the Bad Apples and Miss Amelia

Good-night, Fred.

Rosie Good-night, Bruiser.

Bruiser stands guard

Oh, Polly, I wish you were here now, you'd know what to do. (*She pulls herself together*) I shall stay here until it's light, and when Bruiser's not looking I'll make a run for it. What was it the Professor said, "Don't sleep in Hallowe'en Wood tonight"? I wonder why? Well, it's a good thing that I'm not the least bit tired. (*Yawning*) I won't have any trouble —

staying — awake ... (*She falls asleep apart from the others, lying on her side so that her back is presented to the others*)

Bruiser slides to the ground and falls asleep. Everyone remains sleeping, dreaming their own private dreams, oblivious to the following scene

Spooks enter

Song No 6: Don't Sleep In Hallowe'en Wood Tonight!

Spooks   Don't rub your eyes, don't start to yawn,
Stay wide awake until the dawn and
Don't sleep in Hallowe'en Wood tonight.
Take a short nap and you will find
Horrible thoughts creep into your mind so
Don't sleep in Hallowe'en Wood tonight.
Toss and you turn,
You cry and you moan,
'Cos your very worst nightmares won't leave you alone.
(*Speaking*) Aah!
(*Singing*) Snooze if you dare, you can expect
To remember the things you'd rather forget
When you sleep in Hallowe'en Wood tonight.

The Spooks disappear

The music continues to underscore

During the following scene the dreamers are each visited by their own personal nightmare

A giant honeycake enters and appears to Amelia

Amelia Honeycakes! Honeycakes! Oh how I love honeycakes. Ooh! The biggest honeycake in Appledom. I'm going to eat you.
Honeycake No, Amelia, I'm going to eat *you*!

The honeycake opens and shuts its enormous mouth. Amelia screams in her sleep

The honeycake exits

The Pieman enters and appears to Bad Grub and Fly-Blow, both of whom are having the same dream

Bad Grub Sorry, Mr Pieman — we couldn't find Rosie. I did my best, but Fly-Blow let me down. Put him in the pie not me.

Fly-Blow Don't blame me, Mr Pieman, I was only doing what Bad Grub told me. Take him not me.

Bad Grub ⎫ (*together*) Actually, Mr Pieman, it was all Bruiser's fault. He
Fly-Blow ⎭   should go in the pie, not us.

The Pieman moves to Bruiser and appears to him

Pieman They're right, Bruiser, it is your fault. You had Rosie in your grasp and you let her go. You must pay for your carelessness. *You* will take her place in the pie.

The Pieman exits and disappears. As the Pieman goes, a giant pie appears and comes towards Bruiser, snapping its lid open and shut

Bruiser sucks his thumb and whimpers

Bruiser No, no, leave me alone. I don't want to be put in a pie.

The pie goes. As the pie goes Rosie's parents, Rhoda and Rufus Russet, enter and appear to her

Rufus It's no good, my dear, our Rosie's simply not here. We must move on to another place.

Rosie No, don't go! I'm coming. I'm on my way!

Rhoda Just as you say, Rufus. There's no point in us staying here.

Rosie You must stay! One more day and I'll be there.

The Russets exit

(*Sobbing in her sleep*) Too late — I'm too late.

The Spooks enter and sing

Song No. 6: Don't Sleep In Hollowe'en Wood Tonight!(continued)

Spooks   You say to yourself, this is only a dream,
                        But when you're asleep you can't even scream
                        While you sleep in Hallowe'en Wood tonight.
                        For spooks shriek in Hallowe'en Wood tonight.
                        And ghouls creep in Hallowe'en Wood tonight.
                        So don't sleep in Hallowe'en Wood tonight!

The Spooks exit and disappear

Dawn breaks

Amelia, Bad Grub and Fly-Blow wake up and eye each other suspiciously

Bad Grub I'm starving. How about a bit of brekky? (*He takes the bag of honeycakes and offers them around*) Honeycake anyone?
Amelia Er … not just now thank you.

Bruiser snores

Bad Grub }
Fly-Blow } (*together*) Oh, Bruiser.
Bruiser (*waking up*) What … what is it?
Bad Grub You were supposed to be standing guard.
Bruiser Sorry, Bad Grub.

Fly-Blow spots Rosie

Fly-Blow Here, who's that?

Rosie has her back to everyone. She is still asleep. While she is sleeping, she stretches and knocks off her moustache

Bruiser That? That's Fred, really nice apple. He got here last night When you were all asleep and I told him he'd be safer here, with us, than wandering round this wood in the dark. Did I do right, Bad Grub?
Bad Grub I suppose so, but if he wants breakfast he'll have to pay us for it.
Amelia No, Bad Grub, he'll have to pay me. Those honey cakes are mine.
Bad Grub Yeah? Well if it wasn't for us you wouldn't be here and ——

Rosie stirs in her sleep

Bruiser He's waking up. Would you like to meet him?

Bruiser gives Rosie a shake. She opens her eyes and realizes the full horror of the situation

   Fred, Fred? I'd like you to meet my friends Mr Bad Grub and Mr Fly-Blow.
Amelia (*clearing her throat*) Ah-hem!
Bruiser Oh, and Miss Amelia Crabapple. Friends meet Fred.

Rosie gets up, keeping her back to them all. She takes a deep breath and turns. She extends her hand in greeting

Rosie Delighted to meet you. Bruiser here's told me so much about you.

Everyone stares, open-mouthed at Rosie without her disguise. Amelia, Bad Grub and Fly-Blow give a gasp of recognition. Bruiser looks alarmed

Bad Grub Bruiser, my son, you've done it again.
Bruiser Fred! A bit of your face has dropped off!

Rosie puts her hand to her face and realizes what has happened. She looks for an escape route

Bad Grub Grab her!

Amelia grabs one arm, the Bad Apples take the other

Bad Grub⎫
Fly-Blow⎭ (*together*) Pieman, Mr Pieman! We've got something for you.
Amelia Archie! Are you there Archie ? — Amelia here!
Bad Grub⎫
Fly-Blow⎭ (*together*) Archie?!
Amelia Yes, the Pieman and I are old friends. I forget just how long we've known each other.
Bad Grub Well don't forget this — Bruiser found Rosie —

At this point the penny drops and Bruiser realizes that Fred is in fact, Rosie

   So we're getting the reward.
Amelia No you're not, she's mine!
Bad Grub⎫
Fly Blow⎭ (*together*) Ours!

A tug of war sets off with Rosie between Amelia and the Bad Apples. Each shout alternate cries of "Ours" and "Mine"

We hear the sound of the Pieman's approaching footsteps

Bad Apples (*pulling Rosie towards them*) Ours!
Amelia (*pulling Rosie towards her*) Mine!

They lose their grip on Rosie and fall backwards

   Rosie seizes the opportunity to escape and exits

The Pieman's footsteps get louder as he approaches and everyone quakes with fear. At the moment when everyone expects the Pieman to appear, the footsteps start to fade away instead until they have gone

There is a sigh of relief from all concerned

Amelia Come along, let's get after her!

Amelia climbs aboard the cage/cart. Wearily the Bad Apples take hold of the shafts and set off. But then they stop, look at each other and together let go of the shafts so that Amelia topples out

Bad Grub Oh dear, that has upset the applecart! Ta-ta. Amelia.

The Bad Apples exit, cheekily waving goodbye to Amelia

*Music underscore (**No.6a.**) continues*

Amelia climbs out of the cart, sets off carrying her bag of honey cakes, stops, looks back at the cart, then at her honey cakes. She carefully places the bag inside the cart and exits pulling the cart

Scene 4

At The Crossroads

This scene requires nothing else but a signpost with four arms which could be set in place by an actor dressed as a council work apple. One arm points to Bramleyville, one arm points to Bramley Heath, one arm points to Hallowe'en Wood, and the final arm points to Maggot Marshes

Rufus and Rhoda Russet enter from the direction of Bramley Heath

The following is the scene from Rosie's dream in Hallowe'en Wood

Rufus It's no good, my dear, our Rosie's simply not here. We must move on to another place.
Rhoda (*wearily*) Just as you say, Rufus. There's no point in us staying here.

Rufus puts a comforting arm around his wife and, heads bowed, they exit in the direction of Bramleyville to catch the next strong wind. At the same time, two policemen enter from Bramleyville and pass close by the Russets. However, they fail to notice them as they are too busy enjoying the sunny weather

Sergeant It's a perfect day for the Annual Bramley Fair, Constable, You couldn't pick a better one.

Constable No, Sarge, you couldn't. Oh, I love a fair. I can't wait to see all those rides and side-shows and stalls.

Sergeant Now, now, Constable, we mustn't forget that we are there not to enjoy ourselves, but to uphold the law. To be of help to the public in general and keep a look-out for bad apples and other ne'er-do-wells.

Constable (*disappointedly*) Yes, Sarge.

Rosie enters from the direction of Hallowe'en Wood, carrying her map and the bag of food. She has discarded most of her disguise and looks like a girl. She studies the signpost then looks at her map. She appears confused

Sergeant Bramley nudges the Constable and they approach Rosie

Sergeant Good day to you, miss. Sergeant Bramley and Constable Bramley of the Bramley Constabulary, Bramleyville at your service. Can we be of assistance?

Rosie Perhaps you can. Have you come across two apples called Russet?

Sergeant Russet? Russet? Now that's not a name you hear a lot round these parts.

Constable Bramley!

Sergeant (*sharply*) What!

Constable Bramley! That's a name you hear a lot round these parts. There's Bob Bramley, the barber. Dough Bramley, the baker. Biff Bramley, the boxer. Boots Bramley the ——

Rosie Shoemaker?

Constable No, chemist. Bill Bramley the ——

Sergeant Constable! That will do.

Constable Yes, Sarge.

Sergeant Come to think of it, I did run across a couple called Russet the other day, in Bramleyville. A pleasant if somewhat gloomy pair as I recall.

Rosie That's wonderful! (*She makes to go towards Bramleyville*)

Sergeant But I doubt that they're there now.

Rosie stops in her tracks

They said something about moving on.

Rosie I've missed them. I'm too late.

Constable They might be at the fair on Bramley Heath.

Rosie (*with new hope*) You think so?

Constable Yes — everyone goes to the Bramley Fair, it's famous. That's where we're off to now.

Sergeant Purely in the line of duty you understand. But the Constable does have a point, they could very well be there. Well, Miss, I hope you find these Russets. And if you should ever need our help again just ask for Sergeant Bramley

Constable And Constable Bramley ——

Constable ⎫
Sergeant ⎬ — of the Bramley Constabulary, Bramleyville.
        ⎭

They salute and exit. Constable Bramley re-enters

Constable And then there's Bert Bramley, the burglar …

He is yanked off by the Sergeant

*Music underscore (**No. 6b. & 6c.**) continues*

Rosie studies the signpost, looks first one way and then the other before finally making up her mind. She exits in the direction of Bramley Heath — and the fair

Black-out

SCENE 5

THE FAIR ON BRAMLEY HEATH

This a lively colourful scene with apples milling about and enjoying themselves. There are two tents; one bears a sign which reads, "Gypsy Appolina — I see your future"; the sign on the other tent says, "The Great Stroodle — Magic and Mystery". Near the magic tent is a magician's basket filled with various props and costumes. Two bees have a stall selling "Mrs Buzzybee's Honeycakes". A steam organ can be heard playing in the background

Constable Bramley is dutifully patrolling the area while his Sergeant enjoys a lolly, which he licks when the Constable isn't looking

The Sergeant sneaks off to go on the rides and exits

Rosie enters and wanders around looking for her parents. She ends up by the Magician's tent

Rosie "The Great Stroodle — Magic and Mystery." I wish he could conjure up my parents for me.

Rosie is about to move away when the Great Stroodle, who is really the Pieman, disguised in lederhosen and a big moustache, steps out from the tent and bars her way

The following speech of the Pieman is spoken with a heavy Austrian accent

Pieman *Gutentag, Fraulein. Herr* Stroodle's the name. You wish me to do some magic for you, ya? (*He produces something pretty, a cake, a flower or an ice-cream, and hands it to Rosie*)

Rosie (*taking the item*) Thank you, but I don't think your sort of magic could help me. I'm looking for some apples, but they don't seem to be here.

Pieman Zey have gone?

Rosie I think so.

Pieman *Das* is sad. You know I am thinking, if ze Great Stroodle cannot help ze *Fraulein* zen maybe ze *Fraulein* would like to help *Herr* Stroodle?

Rosie How?

Pieman My assistant, Gretchen, is a naughty *Fraulein*. She go visit ze Uncle and ze Aunt and she don't come back. How can ze Great Stroodle perform his magic without ze assistant?

Rosie I don't know.

Pieman Neizer do I, but zen I am thinking to myself, "Ya, she is just ze right size".

Rosie (*with alarm*) Size? What do you mean size? Right size for what?

Pieman For ze costume. (*He puts his hand inside the tent and produces a girl's Tyrolean dress*) You vill be ze assistant, ya?

Rosie I'd like to help, but I really have to go to Bramleyville, now.

Pieman *Das* is sad also. You make ze gut assistant I zink.

Amelia and the Bad Apples enter

Rosie Oh no!

Pieman Vot is ze matter, *Fraulein*?

Rosie Those apples, I don't want them to see me.

Pieman Zees are ze apples you are looking for?

Rosie No! These apples are looking for me and they mean me harm. I must hide.

Pieman Zen I can help you. You vill hide behind this costume. You vill be Gretchen, no one vill recognize you and you vill help me vid my act, ya?

Rosie Well, I suppose I ...

Pieman Gut, zen we both are happy. (*He hands the costume to Rosie, opens the tent flap and almost pushes her in*)

The Pieman rubs his hands and watches, from behind the tent, as Amelia and the Bad Apples wander around looking for Rosie. Amelia buys a big bag of honey cakes

Bruiser I've never been to a fair, Bad Grub. Can I go on the rides?

Bad Grub No, Bruiser, you'll only be sick. Anyway, if Rosie's not here we'll have to be going. We don't want her getting too far ahead of us.

Fly-Blow Does it matter if she does. We haven't a clue which way she's gone.

Amelia No, but we could soon find out. (*She points to Gypsy Appolina's tent*) Gypsy Appolina will gaze into her crystal ball and tell us everything we need to know. Where Rosie is now, where she's going, and when I'm going to get my reward — I mean, *our* reward.

Fly-Blow Sounds like a good idea, BG.

Bad Grub Yeah, all right, let's give it a go. Come on then.

Amelia Oh no, no, no, no, no! You've no need to come.

A Fairground Barker enters and bangs a drum to get everyone's attention

Barker Roll up! Roll up! The magic show is about to begin,

Amelia Why don't you all go and enjoy the show and I'll join you after I've seen Gypsy Appolina.

Bad Grub OK.

The Bad Apples start to go

Amelia I shall need some money.

Bad Grub What for?

Amelia Gypsies expect to have their palms crossed with silver before they go crystal-ball gazing and I'm broke.

Fly-Blow That's because you spent all your money on honey cakes. Why don't you cross her palm with a couple of those?

Amelia If you're going to be penny-pinching about this let's not bother. Let's go on wandering about the country willy nilly until the Pieman gets to Rosie first, or she grows too big and tasteless to be of use to him.

Bad Grub All right, all right. How much you got, Fly-Blow?

Fly-Blow How much you got, Bruiser?

Bruiser puts his hand in his pocket and pulls out some coins which Amelia snatches away before he has time to count them

Amelia See you later. (*To the audience*) Much later.

Amelia enters the Gypsy Appolina's tent

Barker Prepare to be baffled, bewildered, confounded and confused by the magical skills of the one and only, The Great Stroodle!

The Pieman, as Stroodle, comes out from the tent and bows to the crowd who have gathered round. The Bad Apples join them

The Pieman *Velkom* to the magical vorld of ze Great Stroodle. Pleased you to meet my lovely assistant, Gretchen.

Rosie appears wearing an apron over her dress which has some puff sleeves. She also wears a wig with large, flaxen plaits. She is very nervous, but relaxes when the Bad Apples fail to recognize her

The Pieman begins his magic act by producing eye-catching coloured silks, streamers or flags. Rosie assists

Bruiser Oh, Bad Grub, this is amazing. I've never seen a magician before.
Bad Grub That? That's a load of rubbish, anyone can do that. Hey, Stroodle, why don't you do something really clever? Why don't you make something disappear — like yourself?

The crowd laugh at this

Pieman (*annoyed*) As ze young sir seems to know so much about ze magic perhaps he vould care to help me vid my next trick.

Bad Grub swaggers up to the Pieman and Rosie

Bad Grub Don't mind if I do, Guv.

The Pieman bristles at being called Guv

Pieman For zis illusion it is necessary for me to put you into an hypnotic trance.
Bad Grub *You* hypnotize *me*? I don't think so …

The Pieman clicks his fingers and Bad Grub becomes transfixed

Pieman *Gretchen*, if you please.

The Pieman indicates that Rosie should pass him the contents of the prop basket. Then, with her help, he swiftly fastens a ballet skirt around Bad Grub's waist, places a tiara on his head and sticks a tinselled wand in his hand

How is zat for magic? I turn ze Bad Apple into ze Good Fairy!

He clicks his fingers and Bad Grub wakes up somewhat puzzled as to why everyone seems to be laughing at him. The penny drops when he sees the wand, then the skirt and, finally, his hand flies up to feel the tiara. He angrily tears the whole lot off and stomps off back to the audience to join Fly-Blow and Bruiser, who are finding it hard to contain their mirth

Bad Grub Don't you dare laugh! And don't either of you mention this to anyone … ever, or I'll never be taken seriously as the hard apple of rock.
Pieman Und now for ze highlight of my show ...
Bruiser We've got to watch this.
Bad Grub Not me, I've had enough of stupid magic. I'm going to find Amelia. You coming, Fly-Blow?

Bad Grub and Fly-Blow walk into Gypsy Appolina's tent and exit

During this time, the Pieman sets up a table, which should be strong enough to hold Rosie's weight, and gets Rosie to lie on it. He then covers her with a cloth leaving only her face free

Pieman 'Sawing ze Apple in Half'! (*He produces a very large saw from the props basket*)

Rosie gasps, so does the crowd. The Pieman bends down and whispers to Rosie

(*In the Pieman's voice*) Don't worry, Rosie, you won't feel a thing

Rosie tries to cry out, but the Pieman covers her face with the cloth. When she struggles he simply holds her down. With great ceremony he places the saw over her middle

Bruiser I don't like this, I feel all wobbly.

Bruiser faints and is caught by some of the crowd. The Pieman is momentarily distracted

Pieman Vot is happening?

Rosie manages to throw back the cloth

Rosie (*shouting*) Help! Help! He's not the Great Stroodle, he's the Pieman and he wants to put me in a pie.

There is great commotion. The apples holding Bruiser drop him with a thud

Crowd The Pieman, that's not him? Yes it is, he's in disguise. But he's dangerous. He wants locking up.

One apple from the crowd turns to Constable Bramley

Don't just stand there, Constable, arrest him.

Constable Bramley reluctantly steps forward, somewhat confused

Pieman Sorry, ze show is over. *Auf wiedersehen*!

There is a flash and the Pieman disappears

The crowd gathers around Rosie. Rosie removes her flaxen plaits. Constable Bramley is in a fluster

Constable Sarge?! Oh, Sa-arge?!

He rushes off, blowing his whistle

Bad Grub and Fly-Blow come out of the Gypsy's tent and find Bruiser

Bruiser You'll never guess what's just happened here. That Stroodle, well he isn't a ——

Fly-Blow Yeah? Well you'll never guess what's happened to us.

Bad Grub Amelia's gone. She knows where Rosie is and she's snuck off to find her first and claim our reward. That crafty Crabapple.

Fly-Blow (*looking round*) Where is the Great Stroodle? Did he disappear like Bad Grub told him?

Bruiser That's what I was going to tell you. He's not the Great Stroodle at all, he's the Pieman. You see, he was sawing this apple in ha … ha … (*He faints*)

Fly-Blow and Bad Grub catch him before he hits the floor

Bad Grub What apple?

Bruiser His assistant, the lovely Gretchen. He was about to saw her in ha … ha … (*He faints again*)

Bad Grub Not again. Can't you miss out that bit and tell us what happened next?

Bruiser I fainted. When I came to I could hear Gretchen shouting, "He's not the Great Stroodle, he's the Pieman, and he wants to put me in a pie." Then there was a flash and he disappeared. I liked that bit.

*Music underscore (**No. 6d.**) continues*

Bad Grub and Fly-Blow stare at each other, puzzled. Then, slowly their faces light up as they realize that they have found their quarry

The fairground music slows down

The scene takes on a surreal quality as the action goes into slow motion. The crowd parts and reveals Rosie, sitting on the table, recovering. Having removed her flaxen plaits she is now recognizable. She slowly lifts her head and sees the Bad Apples looking at her. The scene returns to real time

Bad Grub Bruiser, my son, you've done it again, you've scored the hat-trick. Right, let's get her.

Like a silent movie, the music speeds up

The scene speeds up. Rosie is chased by the Bad Apples. She dodges in and out of the crowd and once again escapes

Rosie exits

Fly-Blow Oh no, not again. I've had enough of this. First we find her, then we lose her. Then we find her again, then we lose her again.
Bad Grub Don't worry, Fly-Blow, we won't have any trouble finding her again this time.
Fly-Blow Won't we?
Bad Grub No. This time we take a leaf out of Amelia's book.

Bad Grub points to Gypsy Appolina's tent where the fortune-teller is waiting for her next customer

This time we consult the crystal ball.

They move to the tent and Appolina holds open the tent-flap

You got any money, Fly-Blow?
Fly-Blow You got any money, Bruiser?

Bruiser puts a hand deep into his pocket and produces some more coins

*Music underscore (**No.6e.**) continues*

They all enter the tent and Appolina closes the flap behind them

Scene 6

Meanwhile, Back At The Crossroads

The signpost is set as Act II, Scene 1, by the council workapple

Amelia enters. She is pleased with herself at having put one over on the Bad Apples

Song No 7: Mine!

Amelia   (*singing*) With a clever little plot
I got shot of that lot
Just in time.

I'd better run, mustn't mosey,
Got to lay in wait for Rosie
So she'll be mine.

You can be certain that,
When I catch up with that brat,
I will make her whine.

I'm gonna guarantee
That that reward is all for me.
Mine! Mine! (*Speaking*) Mine!

The music continues to underscore, while Amelia wanders over to the signpost and studies it

What was it that Gypsy Appolina said? "The apple you are seeking will be somewhere foul and reeking." That can only mean one place, the Maggot Marshes!

(*Singing*) I'm gonna guarantee
That that reward is all for me.
(*Speaking*) Mine! Mine!
(*Singing*) Mine! Mine!
(*Speaking*) Mine!

Amelia exits

The signpost is struck

*The music underscore (**No.7a.**) continues*

Scene 7

The Maggot Marshes

A gloomy and unwholesome place shrouded in mist, which can only be crossed by stepping stones. It faintly buzzes with the noise of marsh insects

The marsh is fraught with danger. Maggots lie in wait for any apple foolish enough to cross the marsh. They rise to the surface, smacking their lips in anticipation of a meal

Rosie enters, running and out of breath. She looks back to see if she has been followed. She turns and sees the marsh ahead of her

Rosie The Maggot Marshes! Oh no, I've come the wrong way. (*She peers into the distance*) That must be Bramleyville over there. If I go back to the crossroads I might run into the Bad Apples again, and if I try to cross the marsh I might end up as maggot food. Ugh!

Amelia steps out of the gloom, still clutching her bag of honey cakes

Amelia Like me to help you make up your mind?
Rosie Amelia! But — weren't you at the fair?
Amelia I was, but now I'm here, waiting for you.
Rosie How did you know that I'd come this way?
Amelia Because I'm a lot smarter than you and those smelly, dim-witted boobies I've been forced to run around with. But enough of this chit-chat. You've wasted too much of my time already. Hurry up now.

Amelia grabs Rosie's arm and pushes her towards the marsh

Rosie Why, where are we going?
Amelia To keep an appointment with the Pieman. I hand you over to him, collect my reward and skedaddle before Bad Grub and his cronies show up.

Amelia forces Rosie on to the first stepping stone

Rosie Careful, we could fall in!
Amelia You'd better not! You owe me for all the damage you've done, helping my orphans to escape and ruining my laundry business.

Amelia pushes Rosie on to the next stone and is about to join her when she hears a familiar sound in the distance (**No.7b.**)

Bad Apples (*off stage*) We're the Bad Apples, yeah! We're the Bad Apples.

They sound in good spirits. Amelia panics

Amelia They're not getting a share of my profits. Move!

Amelia tries to jump on to the next stone, but misjudges it and falls into the marsh

Help! I'm sinking!

The marsh gets very noisy

Rosie Here, take my hand. (*She tries to pull Amelia out*) It's no good, you're too heavy. Those honey cakes are weighing you down, let me have them.
Amelia So you can leave me here and keep them all for yourself? You don't catch me out with that one.
Rosie I wouldn't do that.
Amelia Why not … I would.
Rosie But I'm not like you. (*She has another go at saving Amelia*) Please give them to me, Amelia.
Amelia No! (*She hugs the bag of honey cakes to herself*) They're mine.

The Bad Apples enter and watch Amelia, horrified

Rosie But you're being dragged under!
Amelia (*with an expression of horror and indignation*) That Gypsy Appolina didn't warn me about this. I want my money ba — aaaaack!

Amelia sinks into the marsh accompanied by much maggot activity. Rosie is upset, Bad Grub and Fly-Blow turn away in disgust and Bruiser goes all wobbly

Maggot Crabapple, nice. Belch!

The Pieman steps out of the shadows, on the Bramleyville side of the marsh

Rosie You! You were here all the time? Why didn't you help her?
Pieman Why should I, she wouldn't help herself … silly, greedy Amelia. Still, I shall miss her, she was one of my best suppliers. But with her out of the way, I get the goods for free.
Bad Grub Not so fast, Pieman. We're still here and if we get to Rosie first —you have to pay us.

Pieman I hardly think that's likely, I'll beat you to it. (*He steps on to the first stone his side of the marsh and wobbles about*)

Bad Grub steps onto the first stone his side. Fly-Blow and Bruiser reluctantly follow and struggle to keep their balance

Bad Grub Oh, no, you won't.
Pieman (*stepping onto the next stone*) Oh yes, I will.

Bad Grub steps on to the next stone pulling Fly-Blow and Bruiser with him

Bad Grub Oh no you won't.

This goes on until the Pieman and the Bad Apples are either side of Rosie who looks from one to the other in fear

Rosie Stop it! Stop it, do you hear? (*Heartfelt*) I've had enough. If any one of you comes a step nearer I'll — I'll — throw myself into the marsh.

The maggots smack their lips in anticipation

Maggot Pudding! Goodee!
Pieman (*soothingly*) Rosie, Rosie, don't do that. Let me create you a more — fitting finale. Swathed in sugar and spices you would rest in my finest pie dish covered with a pastry lid of butter-crisp lightness. There, wouldn't you prefer to meet your fate at the hands of a Master Chef than in a marsh full of maggots who wouldn't know a gourmet meal from an old boot?
Maggot Old boot?! Yummy!

Granny Smith steps out of the shadows on the Bramleyville side of the marsh. She carries her bag

Granny Nobody's going to make a meal out of my Rosie.
Rosie Granny?! Oh, Granny, thank goodness. How did you know where to find me?
Granny I knew wherever you were the Pieman wouldn't be far behind, and I always know evil when I smell it — so I just followed me nose.

The Pieman grimaces at this unsavoury picture

Fly-Blow (*nudging Bad Grub*) That's who Rosie was living with the first time we found her.
Bruiser Yeah, I remember. She threw things at us — they hurt.

Pieman So, you're the one who raised her. You did a good job, she's a fine apple. (*He puts out a hand to grab Rosie*)
Rosie Granny!
Granny Oh no you don't. (*She takes a giant boomerang from her bag*) This time I'm ready for you. (*She holds the boomerang up*) This one's for you, Joey.

Granny hurls the boomerang at the Pieman. It misses

Pieman Missed me! Ha!
Granny Oh … blow it! (*She stamps her foot in anger, but then an idea comes into her head*) Blow it? Blow it! Blow! Blow!

Granny puffs out her cheeks and starts to blow. She gestures to the audience that they should help. She then turns to the task in hand

Hold tight, Rosie.

Rosie bends down and holds onto the stone. The Bad Apples are unable to do the same as they are all on one stepping stone

The gust of air gets stronger. Perhaps a wind machine could be used here

The Pieman becomes most unsteady. Eventually the Pieman falls into the marsh and is joined by the Bad Apples. Rosie steps across the stones to safety. She joins Granny and they hug

Granny Come on, let's leave this lot to it.
Bruiser Bad Grub, I don't like this. I think something's nibbling me. (*He faints, bangs his head on the stone which knocks him out*)
Bad Grub You're not leaving us to be eaten by maggots are you? We don't deserve that. I mean … we didn't do you any 'real' harm did we, Rosie? In fact, we made a right mess of things. If the Pieman had come looking for you on his own, you'd be pie filling by now.
Pieman (*wearily*) How true.
Bad Grub If you get us out we'll promise to be good apples from now on, won't we, Fly-Blow?
Fly-Blow Yeah, I promise.
Bad Grub And you promise too, don't you, Bruiser?

Bad Grub waves Bruiser's lifeless arm and answers for him

Yeah, I promise.

Bad Grub and Fly-Blow twitch as the maggots nibble. The Pieman makes futile attempts to climb out. Rosie takes Granny to one side

Rosie I think we should get them out, Granny. I know they've been bad, but that was because the Pieman said he'd put them in the pie if they didn't deliver me. You can't blame them for trying to save their own skins.

Granny 'Struth, Rosie, you really are a soft apple. I think they deserve to stay there and rot.

Rosie Granny, please.

Granny I dunno.

Rosie Why don't we ask them to decide? (*She points to the audience*)

Granny Well … all right.

Rosie Shall we leave the Bad Apples in the marsh, or set them free?

Bad Grub and Fly-Blow encourage the audience to set them free

Come on, Granny, let's help them out.

Granny grudgingly helps Fly-Blow and Bad Grub out of the marsh. They then drag the unconscious Bruiser DS

Granny I hope you don't expect me to pull him out as well. (*She gives the Pieman a dirty look*) He can stay where he is. And I hope those maggots chew up every evil inch of him.

Rosie Gran—ny?

Granny No, Rosie! If he gets out he'll be back to his wicked ways before you know it. He can't be trusted.

Rosie But if we leave him here to be eaten by the maggots we're as bad as he is, don't you see? (*She thinks for a moment, then an idea forms*) Why don't we call for the Bramley Constabulary? I'm sure they'll know what to do with him.

Granny The Bramley Con … really, Rosie. How are we going to get them here when they're over there in Bramleyville?

Rosie Perhaps if we shout loud enough they'll hear us.

Granny looks doubtful

Sergeant Bramley! Constable Bramley!

Granny joins in though unconvinced

Rosie
Granny } (*together*) Sergeant Bramley! Constable Bramley!

Rosie encourages the audience to join in too

(*Together*) Sergeant Bramley! Constable Bramley!

This goes on until we hear the Sergeant's voice as he approaches

Sergeant (*off*) Hurry now, Constable. Someone needs our help. One-two, one-two, one-two ...

Music underscore (**No. 7c.**) *continues*

The sergeant enters at a trot, but pulls up suddenly on seeing the Pieman stuck in the marsh. The Constable enters and ploughs into the back of the Sergeant

Well, well, well, if it isn't Mr Take'em and Bake'em himself. Your applenapping days are over. I have here a warrant for your arrest.

He produces the warrant and hands it to the Constable

Constable, if you please.
Constable (*clearing his throat*) A. Pieman, you are hereby charged with doing some very, very, very, very, very, very, very, very, very, very, very — (*he turns over the warrant*) very naughty things. And I must warn you that anything you say will be taken down and may be used in evidence against you.
Pieman Then take down this ———

The Constable gets out his notebook and pencil

— eight ounces of flour, six ounces of butter, half a teaspoon of salt, four tablespoons ...
Constable That's not a statement, that's a recipe.
Pieman I know. I just thought up a brilliant new way with rough, puff pastry and I wanted to jot it down while it was still fresh in my mind.
Sergeant (*furiously*) Constable, cuff him!

The Constable produces a very large pair of handcuffs, puts them on the Pieman and then has to drag him out of the marsh

You're going down, Pieman. And there won't be any pies where you're going either. Just bread and water, bread and water and more bread and water.

Pieman (*starting to lose his cool*) No pies? None at all? Not even on my birthday or as a reward for keeping my cell tidy? Not even the teensiest-weensiest mince tart at Christmas?

As the Constable drags Pieman away, his show of bravado disappears completely

Look here, Sergeant, this is clearly a case of mistaken identity. You've got the wrong Pieman. The one you want is small — with a beard — and a limp …

The Pieman and Constable Bramley exit

The Sergeant has a quiet word with Rosie and Granny

Sergeant Excuse me, ladies, but are they his accomplices? (*He nods towards the Bad Apples*) Should I arrest them as well?
Granny I dunno, Sergeant. You'll have to ask Rosie here.

Bad Grub and Fly-Blow look anxious

Rosie His accomplices? (*She pauses to increase their discomfort*)

Bad Grub and Fly-Blow hold their breath

Actually, Sergeant, I don't think they helped the Pieman one little bit.

Bad Grub and Fly-Blow give a sigh of relief

Sergeant I'd best be getting back to the station. Good day to you, (*He nods to Granny and Rosie*) and to you (*To the Bad Apples*). And remember, if you are ever in need of assistance just ask for Sergeant Bramley or Constable Bramley of the Bramley Constabulary, Bramleyville.

The Sergeant salutes and exits

The Bad Apples, Granny and Rosie move DS *and stand together*

The music underscore (**No. 7d.**) *continues*

A curtain could be drawn behind them to facilitate setting up for the final scene

Scene 8

"This Isn't Poonaworra"

Bruiser remains unconscious and Bad Grub and Fly-Blow are most concerned. They try to revive him

Fly-Blow He's in a bad way, BG. I've never known him faint for this long before.
Bad Grub He's got a big bump from when he banged his head on that stepping stone.
Fly-Blow Bruiser … Bruiser … oh, please, wake up.
Bad Grub Come on, my son, speak to me.

Bruiser begins to come round. He looks about him and is a little bewildered

Bruiser Struth! Where am I? Hey, this isn't Poonaworra.

Bruiser now speaks with a strong Aussie accent

Bad Grub⎫
Fly-Blow⎭ (*together*) Bruiser?

Granny becomes transfixed

Granny Joey?
Bruiser Sis?

Granny turns towards Bruiser. She is very emotional

Granny I thought you were a goner, Joey. I thought the Pieman had took you.
Bruiser (*as Joey*) Hang on … yeah … it's all coming back to me now. I was out in the yard and this big bloke appeared and tried to grab me so I threw me boomie at him, only it came back and hit me instead. I don't remember much after that.
Granny But when I came looking for you, all I found was a long piece of peel lying in the yard. I thought It was what was left of you.
Bruiser (*as Joey, thinking really hard*) Nah, that wasn't me. That was a green scarf I'd been knitting for your Picking Day pressie.
Bad Grub⎫
Fly-Blow⎭ (*together*) Knitting?! Yerrch!
Granny It's good to have you back, Joey.

They hug. Rosie becomes a little tearful

Bruiser (*as Joey*) Good to be back, Sis.

Granny gives Joey a smack round the head

Bruiser (*as Joey*) Ow! What was that for?
Granny For getting into bad company.
Bruiser (*as Joey*) Sorry, Sis, but that was before when I was … when I was …?
Bad Grub ⎫ (*together*) Bruiser.
Fly-Blow ⎭
Bruiser (*as Joey*) Yeah, him.
Granny Well you're Joey now, and don't forget it.

There is an odd noise. Everyone turns to find Rosie sniffing back tears

Rosie blossom, whatever's the matter?
Rosie Oh — I'm just happy that you're a family again. I was hoping to find mine in Bramleyville, but now it's too late. (*She hands the postcard from her parents to Granny*)

A gentle breeze starts to blow

Granny (*reading*) "Catching the next strong wind that blows this way to continue our search for her in foreign parts."(*She pauses, sucks her forefinger and holds it up*) You know, that's the first bit of breeze I've noticed since I got here. There hasn't been a whiff of wind until now.
Rosie (*drying her tears*) You mean — they might still be there?

The breeze gets stronger

Granny I reckon. But you'd better hurry, if this wind gets any stronger we'll all be blown to foreign parts.
Rosie I will. And this time nothing's going to stop me.

Rosie exits

Bruiser (as Joey) rubs his bump

Granny (*calling after Rosie*) Me and Joey'll catch up with you as soon as he's his old self again.
Bruiser (*as Joey*) But — I thought I was me old self?

Granny opens her mouth to explain, but thinks better of it.

Granny Never mind. Well, we'd best be making tracks.

Bad Grub Where are you going, Bruiser…er … Joey?
Bruiser (*as Joey*) Yeah, where are we going, Sis?
Granny Can't you guess?

*This leads into a song and dance number performed by Granny and Bruiser,
with interjections from Bad Grub and Fly-Blow. A backing group of girl
apples could join them if needed*

Song No. 8: Poonaworra

Granny	We're going back to Poonaworra Where the grass is always green And the sky's a really bonzer shade of blue. We're going back to Poonaworra where there's a whole lot of space And a whole lot of bonzer things to do—oo.
Bruiser	You can walk very, very, very, very far, No-one comes near you. You can shout very, very,— * *Optional* (very,very,very,very,very,very,very,very) — very, very loud, No-one can hear you.
Granny **Bruiser**	We're going back to Poonaworra Where we'll croon us a tune Underneath a Poonaworra moon. We're going back,
Bad Grub **Fly Blow**	They're going back,
All	To Poonaworra, worra, worra, worra.
Granny **Bruiser**	Back to the quaint little shack that we call home. We're going back,
Bad Grub **Fly-Blow**	They're going back
All	To Poonaworra. And when we're/they're back we're/they're never goin' to roam.
Bruiser	I'll have such fun digging drains and mending fences.
Bad Grub **Fly-Blow**	I think that Bruiser's gone and lost his senses!
All	We're/they're going back to Poonaworra.
Granny	We don't have the fare so we might have to bo'rra'.

Bruiser	If we don't go today then we could go tomorra'.
Granny ⎤ **Bruiser** ⎦	We're going back to Poonaworra soon.
All	Poonaworra soon! Poonaworra soon. Going back to Poonaworra soon.

Granny, Bruiser, Bad Grub and Fly-Blow exit

*The music underscore (**No.8a**) continues*

SCENE 9

THE TOWN SQUARE, BRAMLEYVILLE

A pretty town square with apples going about their business. One apple looks like an American tourist and is wandering around taking photographs. Sergeant Bramley and Constable Bramley are on duty

Rosie enters and looks around, anxiously

The Policemen move towards her

Sergeant Ah, Miss, those Russets you were looking for ——
Rosie Yes! Are they here?
Constable No, they're not here.

Rosie looks disappointed

Sergeant (*somewhat irked*) No, they're not here. They're there — up in that balloon.

The Sergeant points up at the sky. A basket supported by a balloon should float over the square. If this proves too difficult an effect it could simply be imagined, with Rosie and the company following its course across the sky, or a cut-out of a hot air balloon could be flown across the stage behind a cartoon cut-out cloud

Rosie (*madly waving*) Hey! Hey! Don't float away I need to talk to you. You must come down, it's important!

Granny Smith and Joey enter, followed by Bad Grub and Fly-Blow

Granny! They're up there, my parents, but they can't hear me. What shall I do, they'll soon be out of sight?

The balloon (if used) drifts out of view and into the wings

Granny Hang on, Blossom, I've an idea. (*She rootles around in her bag and eventually produces a boomerang*) It's the last one so I'd better make sure me aim's good. (*She winds herself up, then hurls the boomerang towards the path of the balloon*)

We hear a loud pop, followed by the sound of escaping air

As one, the company watches the imagined balloon's descent. From the wings the basket is tipped up onto the stage, the balloon canopy flops over it

Rufus and Rhoda Russet crawl out in a somewhat undignified manner

Rhoda (*pointing*) That's her, Rufus. I saw her from the balloon. She's the one who threw this. (*She holds up the boomerang*)

The Russets are furious. They march straight past Rosie and up to Granny Smith

Rufus My good woman, what were you thinking of? That was a very dangerous thing you just did. Supposing we'd landed on one of these apples, they'd've been squashed, flat.
Rosie (*softly*) Mother? Father?

Rosie stands behind her parents while they give Granny Smith a good telling-off. Granny just stands there grinning at the Russets

Rhoda Why is she grinning at us, Rufus? Is she stupid or something? That must be it. Only a stupid apple would do something as … er … stupid as that.
Rosie Mother? Father?

Rosie's words finally reach their ears. The Russets slowly turn and discover their long-lost daughter holding out the locket for them to see

It's me, Rosie.
Russets Rosie! Our Rosie!

They embrace. Everyone goes "Aah". Granny blows her nose, loudly. Joey sniffs. Bad Grub and Fly-Blow pretend to be unmoved by the event. The Russets hold Rosie at arm's length to look at her

Rosie Am I what you expected?
Rhoda You're much bigger than I remember, but she has your skin, Rufus.
Rufus And your beautiful cheeks, dearest. How about us, Rosie? Are we
  what you expected?
Rosie Oh yes, you're everything I dreamed of.

They embrace again

  I've so much to tell you …
Rhoda Not as much as we've got to tell you, eh, Rufus? I expect you've been
  having quite a cosy time compared to what we've had to put up with.

They embrace and move away with arms around each other

  We've had to stay in the most dreadful places with awful food and no room
  service.

Rosie grins as her mother witters on

  The three Russets exit

Granny No wonder Rosie could never learn to talk proper, like me.

  Granny gestures to Joey and they exit

*Life in the square returns to normal. A tourist starts to take an interest in Bad
Grub and Fly-Blow*

Fly-Blow What do we do now, BG?
Bad Grub I dunno.
Fly-Blow Everyone seems to have got what they wanted, except us. We're
  not even a group anymore without Bruiser.
Bad Grub Joey.
Fly-Blow Yeah, Joey. And Amelia still owes us that money we gave her for
  the gypsy. Don't s'pose we'll see that again.
Bad Grub Don't suppose we will.

*They sigh and look very gloomy. The tourist, who has been watching them,
approaches*

Tourist I've been watching you.
Bad Grub Yeah, well don't.
Tourist Allow me to introduce myself. The name's Al, but back home they

call me the 'Big Apple'. I like the way you look. You've got something, I don't know what it is, but I bet you'd be a wow where I come from. Can you sing?

Song no. 8b: Bad Apple Theme

Bad Grub⎤ Can we sing?!
Fly Blow ⎦   (*Singing, together*) We're the Bad Apples,
            We're the Bad Apples, yeah.
            We're the Bad Apples.
            'Cos we don't like being good. (*Repeated as necessary*)

Fly Blow We used to be a group.
Tourist Groups are out, duos are in. You heard of the "Fruit Shop Boys"?

Bad Grub and Fly-Blow nod enthusiastically

I manage them. I'd like to manage you, you interested?

The boys nod enthusiastically

I have a contract back at my hotel, so if you'd care to join me there we can get it signed and talk about your future …

The tourist exit followed by Bad Grub and Fly-Blow doing "high fives". The crowd of apples begin to drift off stage and the square empties leaving only Sergeant Bramley and Constable Bramley

The two policemen, who have observed all this, move to C

Constable (*sniffing*) I do love it when everything ends "appley" ever after.
Sergeant So do I, Constable, so do I. And it's ended very appley for the Bramley Constabulary too. We have in our custody the most notorious apple-pieromaniac in criminal history. That should be worth a promotion or two, don't you think? (*He sings*)

Song No.9: It's A Perfect Day (*Reprise*)

Sergeant   It's been a perfect day for nabbin' villains,
                We've never had a better day.
Constable   A crime wave ended,
Sergeant   The Pieman apprehended.
Both   We've lock'd him up and thrown the key away.

Looks like there's only one thing left for us to say:
This is a perfect day for a party.
Come on let's have a party today!

They exit

III. Finale & Exit Music

The music continues with an instrumental reprise of She's Not There, *while
the cast come on to take their bow. The audience are then encouraged to join
in a reprise of* The Happy Apple Song

Company   (*singing*) Don't be a sour face when you can wear a grin.
Be a Happy Apple and you'll win.
If Dame Fortune ignores you or kicks you in the shin.
Be a Happy Apple and you'll win.
And you'll win. (*Echo*) Yes you'll win.
An apple's life is not all honey
Just wear a smile and make it sunny.
Be a Happy Apple and you'll win.

The Curtain *falls*

FURNITURE & PROPERTY LIST

ACT I

Scene 1

On stage: Decorated apple tree. which bears a fruit the size of a small pumpkin
Basket with a frilly cushion
Table set with delicious food
Decorations
Blossom

Off stage: Wrapped gifts (**Party guests**)
Watering-can filled with silvery dust (**Gardener**)
Instruments — guitars shaped like applecores
Music cases

Personal: **Gardener**: apron, with secateurs, gardening gloves in front pocket; label; pen
Rufus: locket and chain, containing picture of Rufus and Rhoda
Pieman: apron; chef's hat; belt with outsize corer/peeler; large pastry shell

Scene 2

Off stage: Umbrella with corks (**Granny**)

Personal: **Rosie**: Locket and chain as scene 1(needed throughout), label

Scene 3

On stage: Two large rustic dustbins with lids. *In one dustbin*: **Bruiser**'s socks, **Bruiser**'s underwear, a giant A-Z, **Pieman**'s Bill of Fare

Off stage: Leaflets with an identikit picture of **Rosie**

SCENE 4

On stage:	Exterior of **Granny**'s cottage
	Garden tools
	Large boomerang wrapped up in sacking
	Old chair. *Beside chair*: basket full of boomerangs
	Barbecue
	Pipe for **Granny**
Off stage:	Tray of food (**Rosie**)
	Small wicker cart/mobile cage

SCENE 5

On stage:	Sticks of wood for **Polly**
	Bushes
Off stage:	Notebook and pencil (**Bad Grub**)
	Small wicker cart/mobile cage. *Hanging from cart:* Instruments as SCENE 1

SCENE 6

On stage:	Gates, with practical light. *Above them*: bell chain. *On them*: Brass plate with lettering (as described page 25)

SCENE 7

On stage:	Gates
	Wash tub
	Mangle
	Line with washing pegged out
	Ironing table with flat iron
	Wood
	Comfortable chair for **Amelia**
Off stage:	Two grey smocks
	Fake beard
	Laundry basket with dirty washing (as described Page 29)
	Bowls of food and spoons
	Plate of honeycakes
	Music briefcase containing song sheets, baton, small harmonica
	Stools or forms
Personal:	**Bob**: notebook
	Amelia: tape measure
	Mr Crispin: college scarf

ACT II

SCENE 1

On stage:	Cottages Bushes
Off stage:	Bag of shopping containing a bread stick
Personal:	**Mr Crispin**: key

SCENE 2

On stage:	Clutter Old make-up box. *In it*: moustache on elastic Screen Clothes chest. *In it*: Male clothes for **Rosie** Cupboard Mantelpiece. *On it*: map, various cards and objects Table set for tea **Blanket for Rosie**
Off stage:	Bag of food Map Cap

SCENE 3

On stage:	Hallowe'en wood
Off stage:	Cage/cart Bag of cakes (**Amelia**) Food, map and cap (**Rosie**)
Personal:	**Rosie**: moustache

SCENE 4

On stage:	Signpost with four arms (as described Page 51)
Off stage:	Map and bag of food (**Rosie**)

SCENE 5

On stage:	Two tents (as described Page 53) *In the* **Great Stroodle***'s tent*: girl's Tyrolean dress, table, cloth

Magician's basket. *In It*: various props and costumes including ballet
    skirt, tiara and tinselled wand; large saw
Mrs Buzzybee's stall. *On it*: Honeycakes
Lolly for the **Sergeant**

Off stage: Drum
Apron, puff sleeves, wig with large flaxen plaits (**Rosie**)

Personal :   **Pieman**: big moustache, a magic trick, coloured streamers or silks
Bruiser: coins
Constable: whistle

SCENE 6

On stage: Sign post with four arms (as described Page 51)

SCENE 7

On stage: Stepping stones

Off stage: Bag of honeycakes (**Amelia**)
Bag containing a giant boomerang (**Granny**)

Personal: **Sergeant**: warrant
Constable: notebook and pencil, large pair of handcuffs

SCENE 8

On stage: As SCENE 7

SCENE 9

On stage: A pretty town square
Camera for **American tourist**
Basket supported by balloon (see alternative suggestions Page 71)

Off stage: Bag with giant boomerang, handkerchief (**Granny**)
Basket with balloon canopy

LIGHTING PLOT

Practical fittings required: lamp over the gates of the orphanage

ACT I, SCENE 1

To open: General exterior lighting

Cue 1	**Fly-Blow:** "... really moving" *The lighting grows darker*	(Page 7)
Cue 2	**Fly-Blow\Bad Grub**: " What?!" *A big shadow appears*	(Page 7)
Cue 3	The **Pieman** exits *Cut shadow effect*	(Page 10)
Cue 4	**Bad Grub:** " ... one of our gigs?" *The* **Pieman**'*s shadow appears*	(Page 10)
Cue 5	The **Pieman** exits *Cut shadow effect*	(Page 11)

ACT I, SCENE 2

To open: Dull, rainy exterior lighting

No cues

ACT I, SCENE 3

To open: General exterior lighting

Cue 6	An **Urchin** holds up **Bruiser**'s socks *Bring up house lights*	(Page 14)
Cue 7	**Bad Grub** and **Fly-Blow** return to the stage *House lights down*	(Page 14)

ACT I, SCENE 4

To open: General exterior lighting

Cue 8   **Granny** holds aloft a giant boomerang   (Page 20)
                 Black-out

ACT I, Scene 5

To open: General exterior lighting

ACT I, Scene 6

To open: Dusk exterior lighting

Cue 9   **Rosie:** " ... we do now?"   (Page 26)
                 Bring up practical lamp

Cue 10   **Rosie** and **Polly** move us   (Page 26)
                 The light gets brighter

Cue 11   The gates shut   (Page 26)
                 Black-out

ACT I, Scene 7

To open: Black-out

Cue 12   **Amelia:** " ...getting up time!!!"   (Page 27)
                 Lights come up on interior of orphanage

Cue 13   Alarm bell sounds   (Page 37)
                 A search light strafes the stage and audience

ACT II, Scene 1

To open: General exterior lighting

No cues

ACT II, Scene 2

To open: General interior lighting

No cues

ACT II, Scene 3

To open: Dusk exterior lighting

Cue 14   **Amelia, Bad Grub, Fly-Blow** fall asleep   (Page 45)
                 Lighting begins to grow darker

ACT II, SCENE 4

To open: General interior lighting

No cues

ACT II, SCENE 5

To open: General exterior lighting

Cue 15   **Pieman:** *"Auf Weidersehen!"*   (Page 58)
              A flash

ACT II, SCENE 6

To open: General exterior lighting

No cues

ACT II, SCENE 7

To open: Gloomy dull exterior lighting

No cues

ACT II, SCENE 8

To open: Dull exterior lighting

No cues

ACT II, SCENE 9

To open: General exterior lighting

No cues

EFFECTS PLOT

ACT I

Cue 1	**Fly-Blow:** " ... really moving." *Sound of heavy footsteps and the ground trembles*	(Page 7)
Cue 2	**Guests:** " What's happening?" *The sound of evil laughter*	(Page 8)
Cue 3	The **Pieman** purses his lips and blows *Wind effect; blossoms swirl around like snow*	(Page 9)
Cue 4	**Granny:** " — it's raining ..." *A strong wind start to blow*	(Page 12)
Cue 5	**Granny**: " — Snow?! " *The wind becomes stronger*	(Page 12)
Cue 6	**Rosie** enters. **Granny** and **Rosie** are whirled around *The wind dies down*	(Page 12)
Cue 7	**Urchins/Bad Apples:** "... be there" *Sound of* **Pieman**'*s footsteps*	(Page 15)
Cue 8	To open Scene 4 *Barbecue smoking effect*	(Page 15)
Cue 9	**Rosie** and **Polly** run off stage *Sound of* **Pieman**'*s footsteps*	(Page 23)
Cue 10	The **Pieman** snarls and exits *Rumbles of thunder*	(Page 25)
Cue 11	**Rosie** pulls the bell chain *The bell rings*	(Page 26)
Cue 12	The gates shut *Clanging sound*	(Page 26)

www.ingramcontent.com/pod-product-compliance
Ingram Content Group UK Ltd.
Pitfield, Milton Keynes, MK11 3LW, UK
UKHW021816150726
7214IPUK00016B/148